10/90

NELL GWYN

NELL
GWYN

BRYAN BEVAN

Illustrated

ROBERT HALE · LONDON
ROY PUBLISHERS · NEW YORK

© *Bryan Bevan 1969*
First edition February 1969
Reprinted June 1969
Reprinted October 1970

SBN 7091 0686 6

Robert Hale & Company
63 Old Brompton Road
London S.W.7

Roy Publishers, Inc.
30 East 74th Street
New York, N.Y. 10021

Library of Congress Catalog Card Number 75-96221

PRINTED IN GREAT BRITAIN BY
LOWE AND BRYDONE (PRINTERS) LTD., LONDON

Contents

Illustrations

Acknowledgements

Once again, to my friend Sir Charles Petrie, my grateful thanks for so kindly reading my manuscript, for making some valuable suggestions, for allowing me to make use of his article in *The Illustrated London News* and for his constant encouragement.

To His Grace the Duke of St. Albans for his kindness and courtesy in showing me his interesting Stuart relics and portraits in his Chelsea home.

To the Right Reverend the Dean of Windsor for allowing me access to study the manuscripts of St. George's Chapel, Windsor.

To Mr. Jack Miller, Stage Manager of Drury Lane Theatre, for showing me round the theatre.

To the Archivist of Messrs. Glyn Mills, Childs Branch, No. 1 Fleet Street, for showing me the ledgers containing Nell Gwyn's accounts.

To the London Library my grateful thanks for allowing me to retain essential works of reference long after the permitted period.

To Mr. Gordon, Secretary of the Army and Navy Club, for kindly showing me their interesting portraits of Nell Gwyn, and for allowing me to study manuscript material in their possession.

To the Director of the State Archives at the Quai d'Orsay, Paris, for allowing me permission to study the original letters of various French ambassadors in London during the reign of Charles II.

To the Librarian of the Royal College of Physicians of London for allowing me access to study some interesting material.

Lastly my sincere thanks to my Publishers, Robert Hale Ltd. for their careful handling of the material and for their invariable helpfulness and encouragement, and to my Literary Agent, Mr. David Bolt of David Higham Associates, for his helpfulness in suggesting *Nell Gwyn*.

To Œnone

I   *The Restoration Age*

EVEN after three centuries Nell Gwyn still holds an enduring place in the hearts of the British people. She is regarded with more affection than any of her rivals, largely forgotten today, who were mistresses of Charles II. For almost seventeen years she maintained her position at Court, delighting the fickle monarch with her gaiety, wit and irresistible charm. He never tired of her as he did of Moll Davis, an actress in the Duke's Theatre, who had pretensions to be a lady. Nell never pretended to be other than what she was; a little cockney of the London streets, who had risen to fame owing to her great ability and fascinating personality. Her very honesty of vice, her utter lack of pretence, her saucy wit captivated her contemporaries as they have captivated us ever since. Even when she was mature—and she matured early in the London streets—she remained at heart a cockney: witty, vital, gloriously indiscreet, impulsive and warm-hearted. Throughout her life she never lost her sense of wonder.

Today she is remembered more for her unique personality than for her achievements. Yet she had a touch of genius. Exactly 300 years ago Londoners were flocking to 'The King's House', or the Theatre Royal, the site of our present 'Drury Lane', to see Mrs. Ellen Gwyn act in the plays of John Dryden and to speak some of the prologues and epilogues in her own irresistible way. She excelled in comedy rôles. Everybody knows she was an orange girl, but it is far less known that she was already a celebrated actress before she attracted Charles II's serious attentions. Nell Gwyn was a patriot. She loved England with all the ardour of a warm-hearted nature, especially familiar places like London, Windsor and Oxford. Her disdainful scorn for foreigners can best be understood when we realize that during her short life she never travelled to any part of Europe. She was insular, and we can forgive her for that. There have been far greater women in history, but none has surpassed her in personality. There are as many houses* Nell Gwyn is supposed to have inhabited as beds alleged to have been slept in by Queen Elizabeth I. She has been the heroine of films, and many taverns are named after her.

Nell Gwyn was already ten years old when Charles II was restored to his kingdom, so it is timely to consider the Restoration Age. We are apt to be far too sentimental about that period. Life for the ordinary man was certainly more brutal and sensual than it is today. As Sir Arthur Bryant has written: "Where the London of 1600 differed from ours was in its dirt and its beauty."[1] With its gabled houses, built of timber and lattice and windowed before the Great Fire, London was a far more beautiful city than it is today. It was still an agricultural town, and cows and sheep might still be seen ambling along its narrow streets. Kensington and Chelsea were still villages, while Knightsbridge, Wandsworth, Islington and Paddington were mere hamlets.

One could smell the rich earthy smells of fruit and beast in the London streets. We are all familiar with the May Day description of Samuel Pepys; of the milk-maids, with garlands upon their pails dancing down the Strand, with fiddlers playing before, and Nell Gwyn, in smock-sleeves and bodice, standing at the doors of her lodging, watching the gay scene. Life for the Londoner could be agreeable enough. In summer, to divert himself, he could visit the Spring Gardens at Charing Cross or at Lambeth, reached by boat, where he could gorge on cherries and cream or a syllabub and tarts. Also popular was Vauxhall, where a citizen could take his wife to eat tarts and cheese-cakes in springtime. When Mrs. Ellen Gwyn, in the part of Valeria, is made to die in the last act of John Dryden's *Tyrannick Love* or *The Royal Martyr*, she suddenly is restored to life as she speaks the epilogue:

> O Poet! damn'd dull poet who could prove
> So senseless! To make Nelly dye for love,
> Nay, what's yet worse, to kill me in the prime
> Of Easter-Term, in tart and cheese-cake Time.

* Recently on 31st August 1967 it was mentioned in the *Evening Standard* that a T.V. composer was renting a small period house in Hornsey Lane, Highgate, once alleged to be occupied by Nell Gwyn.

The audience, remembering summer evenings in Vauxhall Gardens, would be delighted by Nell's reference to 'tart and cheese-cake Time'.

Around London lay an England, unspoilt, still rural and undefiled by development. Horse-matches were held on Banstead Downs, and Epsom and Tonbridge were fashionable watering places. On the South Downs it was still possible to find an old shepherd reading his Bible to his little boy, "the most like one of the old patriarcks that ever I saw in my life".[2] The life of the people, often coarse and brutish, was at least uninhibited and free from artificiality.

There was beauty, not only in the architecture but also in the dresses which people wore. The portraits of Sir Peter Lely have made us familiar with the exquisite satin dresses worn by the ladies at the court of Charles II, but the costumes of the milkmaids and humble folk were also beautiful. An Italian traveller in London in 1669 considered that the women were as handsome as the men. They were mostly tall, "with black eyes, an abundance of light-coloured hair, and a neatness which is extreme",[3] he wrote. The only blemish was their teeth, which were seldom white. An exception was Nell Gwyn, who possessed very fine teeth.

To travel around the narrow London streets could be perilous enough. Pepys had the unpleasant experience of having to leap out of his hackney coach on one occasion, when he was in Tower Street and his coachman turned by mistake into a cellar, "which made people cry out to us and so we were forced to leap out, he out of one, and I out of the other boote".* Rich people owned their own sedan-chairs, carved and lined with silk and velvet. These had been introduced originally from Spain by Charles I, who had gone there as Prince of Wales in 1624 to seek a Spanish infanta for his bride, though they did not come into use until 1634. A monopoly of letting had then been granted to Sir Sanders Duncombe, so as to relieve traffic congestion. The sedan-chairs were carried on poles by liveried servants of the owner, and footmen usually preceded them, with their cries, "Make way for

---

* The 'boot', originally a projection upon either side of a coach, where the passengers sat with their backs to the carriage.

Mylord". Sometimes on dark foggy nights linkboys with torches
of tow and pitch were hired to go before the coach or sedan-chair.
Some were honest enough, others found splendid opportunities
for thieving. Even then London was a noisy city, with the rumble
of coaches and carts on the narrow thoroughfares and the shrill
cries of the apprentices and street vendors. They cried, "Sweet
lavender", "Ripe asparagus", "Fair lemons and oranges". Oysters
could be bought for 12 pence a peck from men with wheel-
barrows.

The majority of streets were unlit at night, so that the criminal
community flourished. Some, however, were lighted till the early
hours by large lanterns, "fixed with great regularity against the
doors of houses, and whenever you wish for them, you may find
boys at every step, who run before you with lighted torches"[4].
Instead of employing vigorous young men as night watchmen,
the authorities often chose poor old infirm people not suitable for
any other calling. If one happened to be abroad after midnight—
not to be encouraged—one could hear their call.

> Take heed to your clock; beware your lock,
> Your fire and your light, and God give you goodnight,
> One o'clock:

Pepys abroad at almost two o'clock in the morning returned to
his house "in great fear to bed, thinking every running of a
mouse was really a thiefe".[5] His was a very understandable terror,
for he had a large sum of money in his house. No police existed,
and honest citizens dreaded the lurking robber. Arthur Capel
Earl of Essex, deeply concerned about the increase of robberies in
the Kingdom, wrote to Charles II during 1673: "They are become
a reproach to ye Government, and look almost like petit rebel-
lions, they going by 20 or 30 in a company breaking open Houses
even in ye day time."

The recreations of the people were crude and brutal. With
insatiable curiosity, Pepys on one occasion visited a new pit in
Shoe Lane where cock-fighting took place. "But, Lord," he
wrote, "to see the strange variety of people, from Parliament-men
to the poorest prentices, bakers, butchers, brewers, draymen and
what not; and all these fellows one with another in swearing,

cursing and betting. . . ." What astonished Pepys was the high betting stakes of these people, though many of them seemed very poor. Sometimes they betted three or four pounds on the result of a cock-fight, only to lose it and bet as much on the next battle (as they called every match of two cocks).[6] Executions were in public, and sometimes 12 to 14,000 people attended; some to gloat over the agonies of some wretched man, some merely from curiosity, like Pepys, who attended the execution of a man named Turner. He stood upon the wheel of a cart "in great pain, above an hour before the execution was done".

Impressionable foreigners considered London a beautiful city, but the intolerable smells and dirt horrified them. Prince Cosmo III of Tuscany, who visited England in 1669, was enchanted by the 10,000 small boats on the Thames. These plied between Windsor and the Fleet, taking people up and down the river or ferrying them from one bank to another. No proper drainage system existed until late in the seventeenth century, and it was the custom to pour slops from high windows on to the streets below. Rivers of filth flowed through this city of strange contrasts. The gutters were dirty, and the people stirred up frequent brawls if they could not walk near the walls. During the winter months a fog of coal-smoke often descended on the streets. Noblemen and courtiers resorted to duels, though they were frowned upon, on the slightest provocation. The ordinary citizen, too, was quarrelsome and turbulent. There are frequent accounts of frays between rival groups of tradesmen. In one fray at Moorefields "the butchers knocked down all for weavers that had green or blue aprons". Actors sometimes struck playwrights, or vice versa, and were sent to prison for a while. Charles Sackville Lord Buckhurst* and John Wilmot second Earl of Rochester, both members of Charles II's court, were involved in brawls. That attractive nobleman, Lord Buckhurst, a rake in his younger days and a poet of considerable merit, was an early lover of Nell Gwyn's. In 1662, five years before he took her away on an unofficial honeymoon to Epsom, he, together with four other gentlemen, had been apprehended and indicted for robbing and killing a tanner named Hoppy.

Rochester, a lyricist of genius but a dissipated rake, was, in

* Later Sixth Earl of Dorset and Earl of Middlesex.

1676, involved in a disgraceful affair, together with the dramatist
George Etherege* and a Captain Bridges.

They were tossing some fidlers in a blanket for refusing to play,
and a barber, upon ye noise, going to see what ye matter, they
seized upon him, and, to free himself from them, he offered to carry
them to ye handsomest woman in Epsom, and directed them to the
Constable's house, who demanding what they came for, they told
him a whore, and, he refusing to let them in, they broke open his
doores and broke his head, and beate him very severely.[7]

Eventually a Mr. Downs, who was attempting to intervene, had
his skull cleft by a sprittle-staff.†

The spirit of Nell Gwyn's Age is symbolized in some verses by
Sir Charles Sedley:

> Drinke about till the day finde us,
> These are pleasures which endure.[8]

Many of the courtiers had endured poverty before the restoration of 'Old Rowley', and with typical zest they were now determined to enjoy themselves. The habits of the English were
certainly dirty. The periwig of William Fanshaw,‡ a lean, impoverished courtier, who held the small office of Master of
Requests, stank to such a degree that his friend Nell Gwyn begged
him to buy himself a new one, so that "she might not smell him
stinke two storeys high when hee knocks at the outward door".[9]
Mrs. Pepys once found in her husband's hair "twenty lice, little
and great".

Coffee-houses were just becoming fashionable. There was one
in Bow Street, Covent Garden, then frequented by literary
personalities and "all the wits of the town". John Dryden, who
had been educated at Westminster School under the famous
Dr. Richard Busby and had become acquainted with Pepys at
Cambridge, often came here. It was later known as Will's. Here
Dryden had a special chair reserved for him near the fireplace in
winter and on the balcony in summer. John Dryden was a great
satirical poet and a dramatist of genius.

* Knighted about 1683.
† A kind of iron bar.
‡ His wife Mary was Lucy Walter's daughter by the Earl of Carlingford,
thus the Duke of Monmouth's half-sister.

London was a city of many taverns. An Italian observer, Count Magalotti, bestowed high praise on the English beers, especially "the delicious and exquisite bottled beers". The nobility preferred to drink the clarets of Provence and Langedoc and those of Naples and Florence. The habits of the English have not altogether changed. "There does not pass a day," wrote Count Magalotti, "in which the artizans do not indulge themselves in going to the public-houses, which are exceedingly numerous, neglecting their work, however urgent it may be."[10] Markets were also very popular. For instance, at the end of August, Bartholomew's Fair was held on St. Bartholomew's Day in West Smithfield. Samuel Pepys would sometimes take his wife there to watch the monkeys dancing on the ropes. On 4th September he saw "a horse with hoofs like rams hornes, a goose with four feet, and a cock with three".*

Such was the London familiar to Nell Gwyn in her childhood, a strange bewildering city, throbbing with life.

* 1663.

Early Days in Coal Yard Alley

NELL GWYN was born at 6 a.m. on Saturday, 2nd February 1650, a year after the martyr King Charles I had gone to the scaffold. This we know from her horoscope,[1] which was cast by Elias Ashmole,* a pupil and friend of the celebrated astrologer William Lilly. The sun, Venus and Mercury are well aspected in Aquarius. Mars is in Pisces (the feet), in harmonious conjunction with the moon. Those interested in astrological lore might derive some encouragement from the grace and brilliance with which she later danced the jigs at the King's House. Unfortunately there is no mention of the place where she was born, a problem which has baffled her biographers ever since. If Nell herself was aware of it, she certainly never revealed it to anybody. It is probable, however, that she first saw the light in Coal Yard Alley, a squalid slum on the east or city side of Drury Lane. At any rate, we know for certain that Nell Gwyn lived here with her mother Eleanor and her sister Rose during her early years.

According to one contemporary writer, Frederick Van Bossen, her father was Welsh, "Thomas Gwine, a capitane of ane antient family in Wales", who had espoused the Royalist cause during the Civil War. Broken in fortune, he had probably lived for a while in Hereford and come to London about 1649, where he had married Nell's mother. Gwynne is certainly a Welsh name, familiar to those who live in Herefordshire or parts of Breconshire and Carmarthenshire in Wales. Unfortunately we know little about Thomas Gwyn. John Wilmot second Earl of Rochester, in his poem a 'Panegyrick on Nelly'[2], relates:

---

* Born on 23rd May 1617 at Lichfield. He later enjoyed the favour of Charles II, who appointed him Windsor Herald.

> From Oxford prison many did she free,
> There dyed her father, and there glory'd she,
> In giving others Life and Liberty.

Nell's mother was certainly a lady of easy virtue, very addicted to the brandy bottle. It seems unlikely that her father was a fruit-seller in Covent Garden Market, since there was no organized fruit market at Covent Garden in 1650. Now that he was almost destitute it is possible, however, that Captain Thomas Gwyn sold fruit in Covent Garden for a while. A Captain Alexander Smith, in a scurrilous and not very accurate book called *The Lives of the Court Beauties* (1715), definitely states that Nell was born in the Coal Yard Alley in Drury Lane. William Oldys, who helped Curll to write the *History of the English Stage*, published in 1741, shared the same opinion.

It is certainly entertaining to conjecture who Nell's real father was. From her physical appearance—for instance her chestnut hair streaked with gold—one would suspect that she had Welsh blood. Her talents as a mimic, her wit and quick repartee seem more Celtic than English.

There is a curious manuscript in the British Museum, which shows that when Nell Gwyn became celebrated a coat of arms was found for her. As Arthur Dasent points out in his book,★ the blazon, in a lozenge-shaped shield, is "Per pale argent and or, a lion azure".[3] The device resembles the heraldic bearings of the Gwynnes of Llansanor and other Welsh families.

A tradition exists that she was born in an ancient house in Pipewell Lane, now named Gwynne Street in Hereford, but there is little evidence to support it. This house was demolished in 1859, and a plaque on the wall of the Bishop's palace garden shows the actual site. Among the Harleian Manuscripts[4] in the British Museum are some ribald verses entitled: 'The Lady of Pleasure or the Life of Nelly Truly Shown from Hopgard'n, Cellar, to the Throne. Till into the grave she tumbled down.' The date 1686 is given, but it is more likely to have been written a year or so later. Here is a verse:

★ *Nell Gwynne 1650-1687. Her Life's Story from St. Giles's to St. James's.*

The pious mother of this flaming whore—
Maid, Punk, and Bawd full sixty years and more
Dy'd Drunk with Brandy in a common shore—
No matter that, nor what we were does shame us,
Tis what we last arrive to, that must Fame us,
Fam'd be the cellar then wherein this Babe
Was first brought forth to be a Monarch's Drab.

Now the title of this scurrilous lampoon is curious, Nell's life described from "Hop Gard'n, Cellar, to the Throne", since Hereford—a lovely city on the River Wye—is celebrated as a hop-growing country. In the printed versions the Coal Yard is given as her birthplace. Could she have been born in the old house in Hereford and brought to Coal Yard Alley, off Drury Lane, in her infancy? It is possible but extremely unlikely.

It is also curious that Lord James Beauclerk,* the seventh son of the first Duke of St. Albans, who later became Bishop of Hereford during the eighteenth century, may have believed that Nell Gwyn was born in Hereford. There were many families named Gwyn resident in that city in the seventeenth century. If a grave doubt exists regarding Nelly's alleged birth in Hereford, that city can certainly claim David Garrick as one of her most famous sons.

One of Nell Gwyn's first important parts in the theatre was Cydaria in Dryden's tragedy *The Indian Emperor*. The intriguing suggestion has been made that Dryden in casting Nell Gwyn in the part of Cydaria—a rôle unsuited to her talents—wanted to allude to her supposed Herefordshire origin. This surely is even less convincing than the other evidence.

The claim of Oxford that the infant Nell was born in their city is also based on very slender foundations. Her elder son Charles by Charles II was first created Baron Burford and the Earl of Headington in 1676.† It has been asserted that these titles were chosen by her because of her family connection with Oxford. However, it is more than likely that Nelly, who sometimes accompanied King Charles II to the horse-matches held annually on Burford Downs, had happy memories of this place. So, she might have suggested to Charles that their son should be given a hereditary title drawn from the county of Oxford, a part of England familiar

* Nell's grandson.   † Later created Duke of St. Albans in 1684.

to her and dear to her heart. As we have seen, Lord Rochester in his poem 'A Paneygyrick on Nelly' mentions that Nelly's father died in Oxford. Anthony à Wood, in his *Life and Times*[5] wrote that her father is believed to have died in that city. This contemporary author traces her descent from Dr. Edward Gwyn, a canon of Christchurch, whose son married a Miss Smith, presumably Nell's mother. The baptismal registers of St. Thomas's parish have not been kept earlier than 1655, so it is impossible to vouch for the truth of this statement.

It is easy to imagine Nell Gwyn as a small girl; with a red streak in her brown hair, half-starved, impish, cheeky and always lovable, playing in the squalid streets surrounding Coal Yard Alley. One must not be too sentimental about her. Her upbringing could not have been worse. We do not know a great deal about Nell's mother, Elen Gwyn, but she was more often than not drunk with brandy and must have been sorely tried to find money to bring up her family of two, Rose and her younger sister Nell. Evidently Madam Gwyn, as she was known, had lax ideas as to morality, and considering her straitened circumstances and the real hardships she had been obliged to endure, we can hardly expect her to be otherwise. In December 1663 Nell's elder sister Rose was imprisoned for a few weeks in Newgate for alleged theft, but, owing partly to the influence of Harry Killigrew, groom of the bedchamber to the Duke of York and son of Thomas Killigrew, manager of 'The King's House' or the Theatre Royal—as the new theatre was called in Drury Lane—she managed to obtain her release before coming up for trial at the Old Bailey.[6]

Rose possessed useful friends, for she also wrote on 26th December to the Duke of York's cupbearer, whose name was Browne, imploring him and Killigrew to obtain her release from Newgate. In her letter she thanked Killigrew and Browne for their visit and pleaded with them that they should obtain her release on bail "from this woeful place of torment". She mentioned that her late father had lost all his possessions in the service of the late King Charles I. It was hard that she should perish in a gaol, since she had never been a thief. A few days later a warrant was given to John Wickham, a messenger, to discharge Rose, who had been reprieved before judgement at the Old Bailey.

Nell's theatrical career was to be closely associated with 'The King's House' and Thomas Killigrew, a boon companion of Charles II. Rose was later married to a man named John Cassells, who seems to have been a professional criminal. However, after having been involved in various crimes of violence, he was apprehended but later obtained his release, owing to influential friends at Court. Later in 1671 he was arrested for attempting to rob Sir Henry Littleton's house. Probably owing to Nell Gwyn's intercession with the King, her brother-in-law managed to secure his release.

We know that Nell's first employment was as a fish hawker in the streets surrounding Coal Yard Alley. Even today there is the faint whiff of fish from Macklin Street—known in Nell's day as Lewkenor's Lane. It was named after Sir Lewis Lewkenor, Master of the Ceremonies at the court of King James I. A district of vile slums, it was celebrated for its brothels, which attractive young girls were inveigled to join as inmates to minister to the sexual appetites of the depraved Restoration fops and others. Lord Rochester, in his poem describing Nell Gwyn as the "anointed Princess, Madam Nelly", relates her early adventures:

> Whose first employment was, with open throat,
> To cry fresh herrings even ten a groat;
> Then was by Madame Ross exposed to town,—
> I mean to those who will give half-a-crown;
> Next in the Playhouse she took her degree
> As men commence at University.
> No doctors, till they've masters been before;
> So she no player was, till first a whore.

The Madame Ross referred to by Rochester was the sinister old hag who kept a notorious bawdy-house in Lewkenor's Lane. No doubt Madame Ross would sometimes visit the fish market, on the prowl, perhaps, for pretty girls to join her bawdy house as inmates. There she would encounter Nelly, who was crying her wares in her childish shrill voice: "Herrings, ten a groat." Her merry laugh, her natural behaviour, ready wit and her very wildness appealed to the shrewd old Madame Ross. Nell was only twelve or thirteen at this period, but we know for certain that she was employed as a servant in the establishment in Lewkenor's Lane, to "fill strong waters (spirits) to the guests".

Later Nell Gwyn in her honest way admitted to this when she was already a celebrated actress. She has been described as always at heart the gamin of Drury Lane, and so she was. She was quarrelling in the King's Theatre one day late in 1667 with Beck Marshall, a colleague, who in a fit of pique or jealousy taunted her for being "My Lord Buckhurst's mistress". Nell retaliated in her courageous manner. "I was but one man's mistress, though I was brought up in a bawdy house to fill strong waters to the guests, and you are mistress to three or four, although a Presbyter's praying daughter."* Davies, in his *Dramatic Miscellanies*,[7] relates, possibly inaccurately, that Aubrey de Vere Earl of Oxford pursued Beck Marshall shamelessly, having been charmed by her acting as Roxolana in one of Lord Orrery's plays. He persuaded her to make a mock marriage with him, which he later repudiated.

Madame Gwyn would have made no objection to her daughter becoming a servant in Madame Ross's bawdy house. Addicted to the brandy bottle as she was, she probably calculated that she would be able to drink more, since the Gwyns were a very devoted family, and Nell would be certain to give her mother an occasional present. Nell was a child of the London streets. With her gay, sparkling temperament she always made the best possible use of life, and she certainly has no need of our condescending pity because she happened to be poor.

A lot has been written about whether or not Nell Gwyn lost her virginity as a servant in Madame Ross's establishment. Although she was never a natural wanton, sex would have come naturally to Nelly. It would scarcely be surprising if the half-drunken men groping up the stairs of the bawdy house in Lewkenor's Lane and sleeping with the girls, whom Madame Ross so thoughtfully provided for them, did not occasionally inquire about the brown-haired girl, always so quick to crack a jest or indulge her witty repartee. Nell was sexually attractive to men at an early age, and it is unlikely that Madame Ross would have

* Probably Stephen Marshall, the Presbyterian Minister in Neal's *History of the Puritans*.

made any protest if any of her clients, despite her tender years, had made a firm offer for her. Sexual intimacy between men and girls was as natural as the coarse oaths of the men frequenting this establishment. It was during her early life that Nell Gwyn acquired that rich vocabulary of oaths, startling enough in such a feminine person, which were to delight Charles II and intrigue Samuel Pepys on at least one occasion. There is a tradition that Nell's first lover was a linkboy, but it is hardly a convincing one.

Sometimes no doubt she would steal away from her sordid surroundings to Brydges Street where a new theatre to be known as 'The King's House' was being built. As she listened to the sound of the hammer and the anvil, perhaps she first acquired the consuming ambition to become an actress. With her quick intelligence, Nell would have realized that her first step must be to apply for a job in the theatre.

In those times Drury Lane was not only a district of slums, alehouses, taverns and bawdy houses, but a luxurious district where many noble families lived. Nearby, in Russell Street, was Rose Tavern, a favourite haunt of players and poets. William first Earl of Craven owned a large mansion in Drury Lane, and other noblemen living there in 1650—the year of Nell's birth—were the second Earl of Salisbury and Lord Howard. An aristocratic lady who had once lived there was Lady Lucy Percy, a daughter of the 'Wizard Earl' Henry Percy Earl of Northumberland. Earlier she had married the Earl of Carlisle, a favourite of James I.

Before discussing the next stage in Nell's career, when she became an orange-girl in the King's theatre, it is necessary to know something of the background to the theatre during the Commonwealth and Restoration eras.

During the eleven years from 1649 to 1660 the theatre was rigorously suppressed, but it is certainly untrue to say that plays entirely stopped when Oliver Cromwell was Protector of England. Naturally the Puritans and the city authorities were opposed to the theatre, and their venom was also directed against the actors themselves, who were often "whipped at the cart's tail"[8] or fined and imprisoned. So were the spectators who were bold enough to attend the performances. For instance, on 11th February 1648, when Charles I was still king, two ordinances were pronounced by the Long Parliament, making all actors liable to punishment for following their profession. Almost a year later, just before the death of Charles I, while two actors were playing the tragedy of *Rollo* at the Cockpit Theatre, the authorities ordered the soldiers to raid the premises. The actors were arrested and committed to prison.[9] In 1654 the authorities grew so alarmed concerning the frequent performances of plays, that during February of that year "instructions were given for suppressing of a wicked sort of people called Hectors, and Playes, and other wicked disorders; and larger power will bee given if need require". During this year plays were so regularly produced at the Red Bull Inn by the Roscians that Puritan troops would raid the inn in the middle of a performance and carry away the actors to a magistrate and to prison.[10] During a raid in December 1654, a play entitled *Wit without Money* was being performed.

At the outbreak of the Civil War many of the actors joined the army. Charles Hart, for instance, who was to become a famous actor during the Restoration era as a member of 'The King's House' in Thomas Killigrew's company, joined Prince Rupert's regiment as a lieutenant of horse under Sir Thomas Dallison. Hart was a great-nephew of William Shakespeare. His father, William Hart, was the eldest son of Shakespeare's sister Joan. He learnt his craft in boyhood, being apprenticed to Richard Robinson, a well-known actor. In his early years Hart often played female parts, for instance that of the Duchess in Shirley's tragedy *The Cardinal*. After the defeat of King Charles I, Hart gained further experience in his profession, sometimes playing at the Cockpit.

One beneficial result from the Commonwealth era was the abolition of baiting bears and bulls, a senseless and brutal sport which had degraded even the spectators. Troopers were sent to the Bear Garden and ordered to shoot the seven bears which were retained for that sport.

Indeed England was a joyless country under Commonwealth rule, and our nation has never cared for dictators. Cromwell even ordered that the Spring Gardens at Vauxhall should no longer be a rendezvous for the gallants and their ladies. The

Puritans regarded morris dancing as a heinous sin and ordered that
the maypoles should come down. Yet there was some entertain-
ment in London. John Evelyn, in his diary for September 1657,
mentions a celebrated rope-dancer known as 'The Turk' performing in that city. For once he did not disapprove. "I saw even
to astonishment ye agilitie with which he performed," he wrote.
A year before the Restoration, however, Evelyn reluctantly
attended a new opera, and, with his puritanical instincts, it is
scarcely surprising if he reproaches himself for being present. "It
was after ye Italian way, in recitative music and sceanes," wrote
the diarist. "I being engag'd with company could not decently
resist the going to see it, tho' my heart smote me for it."[11] Since
grave dangers engulfed England, Evelyn considered that it was
morally wrong for such a vanity to be permitted. This opera was
probably one produced by Sir William Davenant, in which the
cruelty of the Spaniards in Peru was expressed by instrumental and
vocal music. Cromwell would surely not have minded the
propaganda against this nation. Another opera produced by
Davenant before the Restoration was *The Siege of Rhodes*. Although six of the seven performers in this lyric drama were men,
there was one woman in the cast, Mrs. Coleman, who took the
part of Ianthe and has the distinction of being the first woman to
sing or chant on the English stage.

When Charles II was restored to his kingdom in May 1660,
and England once again became a land of joy, there was, among
the crowd of courtiers who walked about the decks of *The Royal
Charles*,* a man called Thomas Killigrew. To Pepys, who
encountered him on this ship, he seemed "a merry droll, but a
gentleman of great esteem with the King", for he was an amusing
companion, with a fondness for merry stories. He certainly
enjoyed considerable license with his master, for he once told him
some years later that "he was going to hell to fetch back Oliver
Cromwell, that he may take some care of the affairs of England,
for his successor takes none at all". He may be described as
Charles II's jester, though during the Commonwealth he had
held the post of the King's Resident in Venice.

In his boyhood this son of Sir Robert Killigrew had developed

* The ship known as *The Naseby* had been rechristened *The Royal Charles*.

a passion for the stage. Even as a child he would resort to the Red Bull Inn, and when the manager asked for boys to volunteer for the purpose of impersonating devils, young Killigrew was eager to do so. This attractive personality is of importance in Nell Gwyn's biography, for he later became manager of 'The King's House', where she played during her six years on the English stage. Killigrew was already aged 48 in 1660 when he became a groom of the bedchamber to Charles II. Sir Richard Bulstrode relates an amusing story about Charles II and Tom Killigrew. On one occasion the King was being shaved by his barber, while Killigrew stood near a window, studying a book of his own plays. The King darted a lazy glance at his friend. "Tom," he remarked. "What account will you give at the Day of Judgement of all the idle words in that book?" "Why, truly," replied the Court Jester. "I shall give a better account of all the idle words in this book, than Your Majesty shall do of all your idle promises and more idle patents, which have undone many, but my idle words in this book have undone nobody."[12] The King was not offended.

While Charles II, on a day in late May 1660, was assuring the Mayor of Dover that the Bible was the book he loved best in the world, Nell Gwyn was a merry little girl of ten, running wild in the streets off Drury Lane. Who could ever be so fanciful as to believe that their destinies would ever meet? But even a girl of such a tender age would be conscious of the joy of the people in the London taverns, the release of tension after years of suppression, the toasting of 'The Black Boy' in tankards of golden beer and the license, which ran through the streets like blood.

King Charles II, when he returned from his exile, had acquired an intelligent taste for the drama, especially for the satires of Molière and the tragedies of Corneille. Gerard Langbaine considered that he was "an undeniable judge in Dramatick Arts". He was an avid theatre-goer throughout his reign, and so were many of his courtiers. Less than three months after ascending the throne, Charles II empowered his crony Tom Killigrew and Sir William Davenant to form two separate companies of players and to purchase, build or hire at their own expense, and in suitable positions, two theatres "for the representation of Tragedies, comedies, plays, operas, and all other entertainments of that nature, in convenient places". In such a way did the King's Company and the Duke's Company come into being.

Killigrew and the principal actors in his company, including Charles Hart, obtained from the Earl of Bedford a lease* for forty-one years of a piece of ground, which lay in the parishes of St. Martin-in-the-Fields and St. Paul's Covent Garden.[13] It was known by the name of the Rideing Yard. One of the conditions of the lease provided that 1,500 pounds were to be spent in building a theatre, and a rent of fifty pounds for the ground. The theatre was 112 feet in length from east to west and fifty-nine in breadth from north to south. It is on the actual site of our present Drury Lane Theatre, and the first of the four theatres to be subsequently built on this site,† but it was known in the Restoration period as 'The King's House' or Theatre Royal. The actors were the King's servants, and Charles II was the arbiter in their disputes. Killigrew also started a training school for the King's players at the Barbican. When Pepys visited the Nursery (as he called it), he was not too disappointed by the acting.

Sir William Davenant organized a company of his own, and the actors played firstly at Salisbury Court in Fleet Street and afterwards in Portugal Row, Lincoln's Inn Fields. The formation of a rival company at least made for healthy competition, Davenant's company was known as the Duke's Company, because it was patronized by James Duke of York, the King's younger brother. In 1662 it was first provided that a new profession would be made available to women, an important innovation in the theatre. Until then women's parts were usually played by men. Both Charles Hart and Edward Kynaston in their early careers often took the parts of women on the stage.

Charles II provided in the Drury Lane Patent:

and we do likewise permit and give leave that all women's parts to be acted in either of the said two companies for the time to come, may be performed by women. So long as these recreations, which, by reason of the abuses aforesaid were scandalous and offensive, may

* Lease is dated 20th December 1661.

† First theatre 7th May 1663; second theatre 26th March 1674; third theatre 12th March 1794; fourth theatre 10th October 1812.

by such reformation be esteemed not only harmless delights but useful and instructive representations of human life to such of our good subjects as shall resort to the same.

As he read through this document a humorous smile must have lightened the harsh lines on Charles' sardonic, but attractive face.

It was at the King's suggestion that the two managers, Tom Killigrew and Sir William Davenant, should divide the dramatic literature which then existed, for no copyright rested in any of the dramatic works that were available. Killigrew was fortunate enough to secure most of the plays of Ben Jonson, such as *The Alchemist, Bartholomew Fair, Volpone, Every Man in his Humour* and *Cataline's Conspiracy*. He also obtained all the works of Beaumont and Fletcher, which were exceedingly popular with Restoration audiences. The sensible plan of dividing the plays of Shakespeare was resorted to. While Tom Killigrew managed to obtain *Julius Caesar, A Midsummer Night's Dream, Othello, Henry IV* and *The Merry Wives of Windsor,* Davenant obtained the right to produce *Romeo and Juliet, Henry the Eighth, King Lear, Hamlet, Macbeth* and *The Tempest.* Sir William Davenant had one advantage over his rival, since Thomas Betterton—the greatest actor of them all—was a leading actor in the Duke's Company.

The first 'King's House' (Drury Lane) was built almost entirely of wood, consequently a danger always existed that it might be destroyed by fire. There were no stalls in the Restoration theatre, and the floor of the house was occupied mainly by the pit. It was fairly comfortable, and the backless benches were covered with matting, but in rainy weather the glazed cupola over the pit could not protect the audience from the rain or hail. The boxes and the middle and upper galleries were reasonably adequate. For the Restoration theatre-goer prices of admission were half a crown for the pit, one and six for the middle gallery on the second tier, and four shillings for the boxes on the first tier. The noisiest section of the theatre was the upper gallery, where the footmen and other servants of the nobility were admitted free during the last act. The plays usually began at three o'clock in the afternoon until about 1690, in the time of Congreve, when performances commenced an hour later. The stage must have presented an attractive appearance, being illuminated by wax candles on sconces. There was music in the Restoration theatre. For instance, Tom Killigrew provided an orchestra, which played muted music in a recess below the stage.

Behind the stage was a kind of improvised scene room, where properties were kept. It was customary for the actors and actresses to wait here for their cues. Above were various tiring-rooms, divided into 'the women's Shift' and 'the men's Shift'. In the basement of Drury Lane Theatre today is a small room sometimes known as Nell Gwyn's dressing-room,[14] though it is to be doubted. However, the walls of this room and of the basement are definitely those of the original building.* The leading actors and actresses were usually provided with small private rooms for their own use. These were simply furnished with various necessities, such as one or two chairs, small mirrors, a table, candlesticks, chamber pots and close stools. As we shall see, there was no difficulty for a Restoration rake, such as Charles Sackville Lord Buckhurst, or John Wilmot Earl of Rochester, to penetrate behind the scenes to visit some favoured actress, either in a tiring-room or in a private room.

During his visit to London in April 1669, Prince Cosmo III of Tuscany attended the Theatre Royal, to see a comedy and a performance of ballet. Seated in His Majesty's box he richly enjoyed this experience.

> The Theatre is nearly of a circular form [wrote Count Lorenzo Magalotti], surrounded, in the inside, by boxes separated from each other, and divided into several rows of seats, for the greater accommodation of the ladies and gentlemen, who in conformity with the freedom of the country, sit together indiscriminately. . . .
> The scenery is very light, capable of a great many changes, and embellished with beautiful landscapes.

The Prince was delighted by the lively music played before the comedy began.

The noise in the Restoration playhouse was often almost intolerable. Thomas Betterton once complained that the voices of the spectators "put the very players out of countenance", though

* I was recently shown round this fascinating old theatre by Mr. Jack Miller, the stage manager.

audiences were silent enough when he was on the stage. Nell Gwyn too, at the height of her brief career, when she was speaking the epilogues or prologues in Dryden's plays or taking the part of Florimel in *Secret Love*, could command silence from the unruly audience. Yet those present at the theatre, if a play displeased them, thought nothing of making audible criticisms. On one occasion that inveterate playgoer Samuel Pepys, sitting near Sir Charles Sedley at a dull play, *The Generall*, was highly delighted when that witty man made some pertinent comments about the badness of the play. On another occasion, however, Sedley annoyed Pepys by carrying on a spirited conversation with "two talking ladies", though Pepys' annoyance was somewhat tempered by the wit of Sedley's discourse. It was at a play entitled *The Mayd's Tragedy* at 'The King's House'. "And one of the ladies would, and did sit with her mask on, all the play, and being exceedingly witty as ever I heard woman, did talk most pleasantly with him."*

Our Victorian forebears regarded with horror the debauched behaviour of the Restoration courtiers—and indeed there is much to nauseate us today. Many of them, however, despite their sexual irregularity, possessed a wide culture and outstanding creative ability. Such were George Villiers second Duke of Buckingham,† a bounder and a rake but a talented playwright, and Sir Charles Sedley, Charles Sackville Lord Buckhurst, and George Etherege adorned the court of Charles II. Yet it is a false picture to suggest that people in the country aped the behaviour of the courtiers of Charles II. For the most part Englishmen were honest, sober and god-fearing. The exhibitionism of the courtiers was largely a reaction and revolt from the Puritanism which had preceded the Restoration age. Even in Whitehall there were a few chaste women of fashion.

On one dark rainy afternoon in February 1667, Samuel Pepys attended a performance of a new play by George Etherege called *She Would if she Could* at the Duke of York's House. It happened that, after the play, Pepys ventured into the pit to search for his

* 18th February 1666.
† George Villiers married to a daughter of Sir Thomas Fairfax, one of Cromwell's Generals.

wife. Whilst waiting for the rain to stop, he overheard an animated conversation between His Grace of Buckingham, Etherege and the others, "who had openly sat in the pit". Etherege was complaining of the bad acting. It is this intellectual curiosity which renders the Restoration Age so fascinating.

Soon after the Restoration of Charles II a brilliant group of literary courtiers, called 'The Merry Gang' by Andrew Marvell, came to the fore.[15] These included such personalities as George Villiers, second Duke of Buckingham, John Sheffield Earl of Mulgrave and Charles Sackville Lord Buckhurst. Later, George Etherege and John Wilmot second Earl of Rochester joined the circle. Many of the courtiers were aristocrats, coming from a privileged class. They were drunkards and indulged in whoring, partly because they had too much money in their pockets and too much time on their hands.

On 7th May 1663—a momentous day for the English theatre—Thomas Killigrew opened his new theatre, 'The King's House', with a popular play by Beaumont and Fletcher called *The Humourous Lieutenant*. There was a strong cast, including Charles Hart in the part of Demetrius and Michael Mohun playing the part of Leontius. Ann Marshall took the part of Celia, thus being the first lady to act on the stage of Drury Lane. Nell Gwyn later played the great part of Celia when this play was revived in February 1666, "and did it pretty well" in the opinion of Samuel Pepys, no mean critic, though he considered it a silly play. It is tempting to imagine Nell—a girl of thirteen—on this afternoon in springtime watching the jostling crowds surge into the pit and the galleries. Perhaps, too, she waited amid seething excitement to see the arrival of the actors, of handsome Charles Hart with his rich sonorous voice and of little Michael Mohun, always so sensitive, modest and such a fine actor.

III   *Orange Girl and Actress*

But first the Basket her fair arm did suit,
Laden with Pippins and Hesperian Fruit.
This first step rais'd, to the wond'ring Pit she sold,
The lovely Fruit smiling with streaks of Gold.*

W E KNOW for certain that soon after the opening of 'The King's House', Nell Gwyn obtained a position there as an orange-girl. She would have stood in the pit, with her back to the stage and with a basket of oranges covered with vine leaves on her arm. In her sauciest manner she would cry to the spectators, "Oranges, will you have any oranges", and with many a witty jest and exchange of banter with the Restoration fops who flirted with her. She sometimes indulged freely in cursing, both as orange-wench and later as actress. The curious expressions she used must have astonished and delighted some ears. "Anybody might know she had been an orange-wench by her swearing," her rival, Louise de Kéroualle, was later to say of her, with a disdainful pout.

It seems possible that Rose, Nell's elder sister, helped her to obtain this position. We have seen that whilst in prison Rose had applied to Harry Killigrew, so that he might use his influence to secure her release from Newgate. Once she had regained her liberty it would be easy for her to obtain a pass into 'The King's House'. There she would have become acquainted with a celebrated character known as Orange Moll, whose real name was Mrs. Mary Meggs. She was in charge of the orange-girls. It is very likely that Rose Gwyn introduced her sister Nell to Orange Moll, and, with the shrewdness of her kind, Mrs. Meggs would have

* From a 'Panegyrick on Nelly' by Lord Rochester.

sensed great possibilities in the pretty girl who came to her for employment.

Mary Meggs was a widow, and her influence in the Theatre Royal was not to be despised. She knew all the gossip of the theatre, whether or not an actress or orange-girl was sleeping with a nobleman or an actor, and was well apprized as to theatrical intrigues. Naturally Pepys was acquainted with Orange Moll. It was from her that he ascertained that Lord Buckhurst had left Nell Gwyn after their liaison had ended in the late summer of 1667. Orange Moll was on several occasions of service to Pepys, bearing messages to him from his actress friend Mrs. Knipp when she needed an assignation. Orange Moll lived in the parish of St. Paul's, Covent Garden, conveniently near her work. On one occasion, when a gentleman in the audience seemed to be choking himself to death with some oranges he had eaten, Orange Moll, with considerable presence of mind, pushed the obstruction down his throat. Sometimes she indulged in quarrels, and after one sharp altercation with Beck Marshall, a leading actress of 'The King's House', the Lord Chamberlain ordered Moll's arrest. Orange Moll held a license to sell oranges and other fruit which was to last for thirty-nine years. On 10th February 1663 the owners and shareholders in the theatre, including Tom Killigrew, Michael Mohun, Charles Hart and Nicholas Burt, granted to her a payment of a hundred pounds, full, free and sole liberty, license and power and authority to vend, utter and sell oranges, lemons, fruit, sweetmeats and all manner of fruiterer's and confectioner's wares. For this privilege Mrs. Meggs was obliged to pay six shillings and eightpence every acting day.

Oranges cost sixpence each, and a gentleman would never haggle about the price. An unscrupulous orange-girl once told Mr. Pepys that he owed her for a dozen oranges, which was absolutely untrue. "For quiet," however, Pepys immediately "bought four-shillings' worth from her at sixpence a-piece". Ladies sitting in the pit usually wore vizards or masks.

Nell Gwyn was not destined to remain an orange-girl for more than eighteen months. It is related that a rich man called Robert Duncan took[7] a fancy to Nelly. No doubt he was enchanted by her saucy wit, her fine figure and the smallness of her feet.

According to Oldys, in the account of her life which he wrote for Curll's *History of the English Stage*, Robert Duncan, a rich merchant, became her first patron and used his influence to introduce her to the stage. George Etherege, in his bitter satire, *The Lady of Pleasure*, relates that, to repay her benefactor in later life, Nell Gwyn obtained for Duncan a commision in the Guards. Peter Cunningham,[1] however, is of the opinion that Duncan was never a merchant and that he is identical with the Dongan mentioned by the Count de Grammont. "About this time [1666] died Dongan, a gentleman of merit, who was succeeded by Durfort, afterwards Earl of Feversham, in the post of lieutenant of the duke's life guards."[2] De Grammont was presumably referring to the French-born Louis de Duras Earl of Feversham. Whatever the truth may be, there is no means of knowing whether or not Robert Duncan or Dongan was Nelly's lover.

According to Colley Cibber,[3] it was Charles Hart who introduced Mrs. Gwyn upon the stage, "and has acquired the distinction of being ranked among the lady's first felicitous lovers". Cibber also assumes that Charles Hart succeeded John Lacy, a well-known actor in 'The King's House', as a lover of Nell Gwyn, "her Charles I" as she later referred to him.

We have already mentioned the bawdy verses about Nelly entitled 'The Lady of Pleasure' or the 'Life of Nelly Truly shown from Hopgard'n Cellar to the Throne'.[4]

> Then enter Nelly on the public stage
> Harlot of harlots, Lais of the age
> But there what Lacy's fumbling age abus'd
> Hart's sprightly vigour more robustly us'd.

It is related that John Lacy taught Nelly how to dance, and that Hart moulded and trained her for the stage. Lacy was a superb dancer, for when he first came to London in 1631 he had been apprenticed to a dancing master named John Ogilvy. Like Hart, John Lacy was a handsome man, being "of a rare shape of body and good complexion". During the Civil War he served in the army as a lieutenant and quarter-master under Colonel Charles Gerard, later Earl of Macclesfield. Lacy was not only an accomplished actor, excelling in parts such as Falstaff, but he was also a dramatist. He wrote a play called *The Old Troop*, or *Monsieur*

Raggou, a witty satire concerning the cavalier troops billeted in the country. Nell Gwyn may have acted in this play, but it is by no means certain. Lacy seemed to have specialized in the parts of fat men, for he played Pinguister in the Honourable James Howard's *All Mistaken* or *The Mad Couple*. Nell created the part of the madcap Mirida in this play.

Charles II highly esteemed Lacy, and he was his favourite actor. He had been painted by Michael Wright, and according to Evelyn this portrait was hung in the King's dining-room at Windsor. The diarist considered it Wright's best portrait, painted as he was "in three dresses", as "a gallant, a Presbyterian Minister, and a Scots Highlander in his plod". However, on at least one occasion Charles was very angry with Lacy for abusing the Court. Lacy had a comic part in a serious play called *The Change of Crownes* by the Hon. Edward Howard.* Pepys, who was present in 'The King's House' on 15th April 1667, relates: "Lacy did act the country-gentleman come up to Court, who do abuse the Court with all the imaginable wit and plainness about selling of places, and doing everything for money." The King was so offended that he ordered Lacy to be confined in the porter's lodge in Whitehall. On another occasion Lacy rashly told the Hon. Edward Howard that "he was more a fool than a poet". As he was a gentleman by birth, Howard could hardly stomach such insolence from a mere actor. He therefore slapped him in the face with his glove. Thus provoked, Lacy attempted to use his stick. Howard then complained to the King, who ordered the actor to be confined to the porter's lodge at Whitehall for a few days.

The critic Langbaine may have had too exalted an opinion of Lacy, for he wrote of him: "He performed all parts that he understood to a miracle, insomuch that I am apt to believe, that as this age never had, so the next never will have his equal, at least not his superior."[5]

Nell Gwyn was certainly fortunate in her mentors, for Charles Hart was also an extremely fine actor, excelling in many Shakespearean rôles such as Hotspur, Brutus and Othello. Hart always asserted that it was impossible for a player to act with grace unless

---

* A younger son of the first Earl of Berkshire, brother to Sir Robert Howard and brother-in-law to John Dryden.

he forgot that he was before an audience. He was as successful in comedy as tragedy, playing many leading parts in the works of Dryden, Ben Jonson and Beaumont and Fletcher. He would have found Nell an apt pupil, with a wonderful talent for mimicry and memorizing her lines. She was completely lacking in self-consciousness and without any inhibitions. Actor-managers soon became aware that here was an actress with a unique personality. Might she not be used to speak the prologues and epilogues in the plays of the rising star, John Dryden? Nell was absolutely illiterate, for she could not write her own letters and was only capable of signing some document or deed with her initials 'E.G.' But she could no doubt read easily enough a part in a play. If she sometimes forgot a word or a line, she would have experienced no difficulty in finding a witty substitute.

Nell Gwyn at 16 or 17 was an enchanting girl. She was below middle height, slender enough, with a lovely figure, exquisite legs and tiny feet. Her hair was chestnut, and its tresses fell most becomingly over her beautiful shoulders. Her eyes were hazel, like pools reflected in sunshine, and when she smiled or laughed, which often happened, she revealed very fine white teeth. Perhaps her most attractive features were her dark eyelashes, which contrasted agreeably with her hair, unusual for a girl of plebeian origin. Her hands too were small and much admired, while her voice was sweet and caressing.

Nell Gwyn first appeared in an important play in John Dryden's *The Indian Emperor* or *The Conquest of Mexico by the Spaniards*, produced at 'The King's House' or the Theatre Royal in the spring of 1665. She was hardly 15 at the time. Yet she was expected to play the tragic part of Cydaria, daughter of the Emperor Montezuma. She was woefully miscast in this play, but it has never been sufficiently emphasized that her career on the English stage only lasted a bare six years. Even if her gifts were for comedy rather than tragedy, and she herself admitted her dislike of playing serious parts, it would be expecting too much of a young actress to reveal great talent as a tragedian in her first play. When speaking the epilogue (1668) in *The Great Favourite* or the *Duke of Lerma*, a play partly written by Sir Robert Howard and certainly his best one, Nell said:

I know you in your hearts,
Hate serious plays—as I hate serious parts.

Again, in the epilogue to John Dryden's *Tyrannick Love*, she is made to say:

I die
Out of my calling in a tragedy.

Her temperament was too gay and merry for tragedy. Dryden was now 34, in the full flower of his poetical and dramatic genius. In 1663 he married Lady Elizabeth Howard, eldest daughter of the Earl of Berkshire. Earlier he had been elected a member of the Royal Society and was much esteemed by Charles II. However, his early work, *The Wild Gallant*, when it was first performed at the old playhouse in Vere Street in February 1663 was a failure.* He later collaborated with his brother-in-law Sir Robert Howard in a play called *The Indian Queen* about Montezuma, which enjoyed a moderate success.

The Indian Emperor is surely one of Dryden's finest tragedies. Much of the poetry, in rhymed couplets, is beautiful, and the drama is powerful. The play has deep significance for us, because Nell was given an important part as Cydaria, playing opposite her tutor-lover, Charles Hart, as the handsome Spaniard Cortez. It is, perhaps, surprising that a young actress possessing little experience should have been given the leading female part. The audience would have been well aware that Nell Gwyn was Hart's mistress, for they knew everything about their favourite actors. Colley Cibber considered—and he may well be right—that the private character of an actor will always more or less affect his public performance. "I have seen," he wrote, "the most tender sentiment of love in Tragedy create laughter, instead of compassion, when it has been applicable to the real engagements of the person that utter'd it." It is probable that the audience in the Theatre Royal could not reconcile in their minds the gay young actress Mrs. Ellen Gwyn assuming a tragic rôle.

The part of the Emperor Montezuma, Cydaria's father, was played by Michael Mohun, a distinguished actor, who had, like Charles Hart, fought for Charles I during the Civil War and had

* John Evelyn saw it at Court, 5th February 1663.

become a major. He would often refer to his army experience, and he preferred to be addressed as Major Mohun. He was celebrated for his tact and skill in settling disputes between the actors. His modesty too was engaging, for he once gently remarked to the playwright Nathaniel Lee, who was reading a play to him, "Unless I could play the part as beautifully as you read it, it were vain to try it at all." Alibech was played by a young actress named Mrs. Elizabeth Weaver, who had joined Thomas Killigrew's company in the early days. Mrs. Mary Knipp told Pepys on one occasion that Elizabeth Weaver had been one of Charles II's many mistresses. "The King first spoiled Mrs. Weaver, which is very mean, methinks, in a prince," he moralized. Pepys records on 15th January 1666 "that Knipp had taken over Mrs. Weaver's great part in *The Indian Emperor* and is coming on to be a great actor".

When Cydaria's father Montezuma wishes to marry her to Orbellan, an Indian prince, Cydaria exclaims passionately:

> So strong an hatred does my nature sway,
> That spight of duty I must disobey.
> Besides you warn'd me still of loving two,
> Can I love him, already loving you?

Nell has been much criticized for her acting in this play, but it is difficult to conceive that she would have said these lines without feeling. She has not yet met Cortez, (Hart), with whom she falls in love at first sight. Here are some tender passages between Mrs. Ellen Gwyn and Charles Hart:

> *Cydaria:* My Father's gone, and yet I cannot go,
> Sure I have something lost or left behind!
> *Cortez:* Like Travellers who wander in the snow,
> I on her beauty gaze till I am blind.
> *Cydaria:* Thick breath, quick pulse, and heaving of my heart,
> All signs of some unwonted change appear:
> I find myself unwilling to depart,
> And yet I know not why I would be here.
> (*To Cortez*)Stranger, you raise such torments in my breast,
> That when I go, if I must go again,
> I'll tell my Father you have rob'd my rest,
> And to him of your injuries complain.

Cortez: Unknown, I swear, those wrongs were which I wrought,
          But my complaints will much more just appear,
          Who from another world my freedom brought,
          And to your conquering Eyes have lost it here.
Cydaria: Where is that other world from whence you came?
Cortez: Beyond the ocean, far from hence it lies.
Cydaria: Your other world, I fear, is then the same
          That souls must go to when the body dies.
          But what's the cause that keeps you here with me?
          That I may know what keeps me here with you?
Cortez: Mine is a love which must perpetual be,
          If you can be so just as I am true.[6]

Dryden dedicated this play to the young Anna Scott, wife of
the King's bastard, the Duke of Monmouth. He explained his
purpose in writing it in a letter.

I have neither follow'd the Truth of History, not altogether left it:
but have taken all the liberty of a Poet, to adde, alter, or diminish,
as I thought might best conduce to the beautifying of my work. It
not being the business of a Poet to represent [historical] truth but
probability.

Though he greatly admired Nell, Pepys is very critical of her
acting in this play. He saw her in the part of the Emperor's
daughter over two years later when he visited the King's playhouse', together with my Lord Brouncker and his mistress. "I was
most infinitely displeased with her being put to act the Emperor's
daughter, which is a great and serious part, which she does most
basely." What troubled Pepys even more was that Mrs. Mary
Knipp, presumably playing the part of Alibech, sent a message to
him through an intermediary, Orange Moll, after the performance that she would like to speak with him, but he was prevented
from doing so owing to a previous engagement.

He was, however, highly delighted to sit near Nelly on one
occasion in early April* 1665 at the Duke of York's theatre, when
he was attending a performance of *Mustapha* by Lord Orrery, in
which Betterton was acting. "All the pleasure of the play was,"
wrote Pepys, "the King and my Lady Castlemaine were there;
and pretty witty Nell Gwynn, at the King's House, and the

* 3rd April.

younger Marshall sat next us; which pleased me mightily." The 'Younger Marshall' referred to was Beck, with whom Nell was to have a sharp altercation about Lord Buckhurst over two years later. Pepys could not conceal his admiration for Lady Castlemaine,* Charles II's rapacious mistress, who had for several years after his Restoration acquired an absolute ascendancy over the King. By 1664, however, a new star had arisen, the exquisitely lovely Frances Stuart, who had been a maid of honour to Henrietta Duchess of Orleans,† in France. Charles fell madly in love with her and pursued her shamelessly, but she almost certainly never became his mistress.

In May 1665 Nell Gwyn seemed to be on the threshold of a dazzling theatrical career when an ominous event temporarily interrupted it, blighting not only her own prospects, but those of her rivals in 'The King's House' and 'The Duke of York's House'. That dreaded scourge and curse of the seventeenth century, the Great Plague, again invaded London.

The scorching sun beat mercilessly on the parched London streets during the early summer of 1665, making the stenches even more intolerable than usual. Pepys, abroad in Drury Lane on 7th June, the hottest day that he had ever experienced, saw two or three houses marked with a red cross upon the doors, and "Lord have mercy upon us!" written there, "which was a sad sight to me, being the first of the kind that, to my remembrance, I ever saw". Three days earlier the Lord Chamberlain had ordered that the theatres should be closed because of the plague. They were not to reopen until October 1666, when Sir William Davenant produced, at 'The Duke's House', Etherege's *Love in a Tub*.

A biographer is faced with difficulties when he tries to record Nell's activities during the late summer and winter of 1665–66. There are no letters or documents to enlighten us. Here there is shadow and misty uncertainty where we long for knowledge. As Sir Winston Churchill has written in *The Unrelenting Struggle*, "History, with its flickering lamp stumbles along the trail of the past, trying to reconstruct its scenes, to revive its echoes and kindle with pale gleams the passion of former days." Yet it is

---

* Née Barbara Villiers, daughter of Lord and Lady Grandison.
† Charles II's youngest sister—the adored Minette.

fascinating to conjecture where Nell Gwyn went while the macabre pestilence raged in London. We do not really know. Dasent believes that Nell and her mother may have removed themselves to Oxford. It is certain that she left Drury Lane that summer, possibly accompanied by Charles Hart, who would have found her comfortable lodgings in the country. Together they would have rehearsed plays, and at night they would have made love, perhaps with the sweet smell of honeysuckle drifting faintly through the latticed windows of some old inn. Nell was far too kindly and warm-hearted a person not to worry incessantly about any of her friends who had been compelled to remain in the metropolis. As an actress of 'The King's House', she was among the King's servants and was supposed to receive a salary from the Treasury during a time of crisis. We know that the actors of 'The King's House' were obliged to petition Charles II for payment of arrears owing to them in December 1666 when the plague was over. Even the twenty-two musicians of the violin to the King had to petition Charles II on 7th November, for payment of part of their arrears out of the 15,000 pounds provided for His Majesty's servants.

For those who were compelled to remain in London, it was a time of horror. At night the bell of the dead-cart, with the doleful cry, "Bring out your dead", could be constantly heard in the narrow ancient streets. And the stenches of the pest-houses, with the bodies riddled with disease. By 20th June several people in Westminster had died of the plague in Bell Alley, near the palace gate. All those who could piled their chattels and goods into "coaches and waggons", making for the country.[7] It was the poor, as was customary, who suffered most. Edmund Godfrey,* a courageous official who had been obliged owing to his duties to remain in London, wrote to the Earl of Newport on 19th December 1665: "The poor people cry out upon the dearness of fuel and want of employment, by reason of the King and Court having been so long out of town, and some of the courtiers, nobility and gentry forgetting of their debts as well as their charity."[8] However, there were many honourable and con-

---

* Better known as Sir Edmund Berry Godfrey, a magistrate, who was murdered during the Papist terror in 1678.

scientious members of the nobility, like Lord Craven and George Monck Duke of Albermarle, who stayed at their posts in London. When the plague was subsiding in London towards the end of 1666, there was an outbreak in Norwich, which suffered more severely than any other provincial city.

If Nell Gwyn settled in Oxford during the plague, it is intriguing to record that her sovereign visited that city towards the end of 1665. There, in Christ Church, he listened enchanted as Frances Stuart sang French songs to him in her sweet voice, while in Oxfordshire "the pestilence was creeping through village hovels westwards".[9]

By late March 1666, Samuel Pepys was longing for the theatres to reopen, "but God knows when they will begin to act again", he confided to his diary. Owing to his duties as Clerk of the Acts, Pepys had been compelled to remain in London. Lately he had been gratified by a gracious compliment from Charles II. "Mr. Pepys," he had assured him, "I do give thanks for your good service all this year, and I assure you that I am very sensible of it." Now Pepys wished to see for himself the alterations to the stage of 'The King's House' which Tom Killigrew was planning.

My business here was to see the inside of the stage and all the tiring-rooms and machines; and indeed, it was a sight worth seeing. But to see their clothes, and the various sorts, and what a mixture of things there was; here a wooden leg, there a ruff, here a hobby-horse, there a crown, would make a man split himself to see, with laughing: and particularly Lacy's wardrobe and Shotrell's.* But then again to think how fine they show on the stage by candlelight, and how poor things they are to look at too near hand, is not pleasant at all.[10]

Orange Moll, usually well-informed, told Pepys and Sir William Penn on 29th August that the players had begun to act on the 18th. If this is true, it must have been an isolated performance, for the theatres did not really reopen until towards the end of 1666.

On 1st November 1666 the actors petitioned the King that the theatres should be reopened, promising that they would donate the financial proceeds one day in every week to the poor.[11]

* Pepys was referring to Robert Shotterel, who was living in Playhouse Yard, Drury Lane, 1681–84, an original member of the King's Company.

Charles II was willing to grant them this privilege, but the Archbishop of Canterbury insisted that there still remained a danger of infection, and performances were again prohibited. Four weeks later the players offered larger donations for charity and were definitely given permission to act.

Another calamity had occurred two months earlier; the Great Fire of London, which destroyed a great part of the medieval London familiar to Nell Gwyn. The fire broke out on the night of 1st September in Pudding Lane and, fanned by a hot eastern wind, spread to the city. Most of the houses were of wood, which fiercely burned and vomited sparks and flakes of flame to set other houses afire before the wind. And the cries of the wretched people rose amidst the awful roaring of the fire and the falling of masonry and church steeples. The river was crowded with boats carrying the goods and furniture of those able to flee to the water-side. One pathetic spectacle to be seen was of poor pigeons, reluctant to leave their lofts and homes and flying around till many burned their wings and so fell into the flames. To watchers, the sky itself seemed to be afire, and night glowed more redly than the day. The people with their marked xenophobia cursed the French and the Dutch and said that the fire was the work of traitors or wretches in the pay of foreign powers.

While the fire raged, King Charles and his brother, the Duke of York, toiled among the workmen, encouraging them by their personal example. Owing to the King, many churches were saved, and the Duke had the excellent conception of blowing up with gunpowder houses that stood in the way of the fire, thus arresting its further development. When the King commanded the feeble Lord Mayor, Sir Thomas Bludworth, "like a man spent with a handkerchief about his neck" to pull down houses, he lamented, "Lord! What can I do? I am spent: people will not obey me. I have been pulling down houses, but the fire overtakes us faster than we can do it."

When the fire was over, Charles II and Dr. Christopher Wren saw in the calamity a means whereby a new and noble city might arise, free from hovels in dark alleyways and better made to endure. In such a way was planned the rebuilding of ruined streets, churches and public buildings.

IV   *More Celebrated Rôles as an Actress*

O N 8th December 1666 Nell Gwyn was acting once again
in a play by the Hon. James Howard, a brother-in-law
of John Dryden, much to the delight of her many admirers.
It was a play very popular with Restoration audiences, called
The English Monsieur, witty and entertaining enough but not
possessing much depth. It is vastly amusing to think of Nell
creating the part of a rich widow named Lady Wealthy, for she
was not yet 17. It was a part particularly suited to her genius.
Hart played the important part of Welbred. Lady Wealthy's wit
and good humour is very evident in the following dialogue.

Lady Wealthy: When will I marry you? When will I love ye, you
should ask me first.
Welbred: Why! don't ye?
Lady Wealthy: Why do I. Did you ever hear me say I did?
Welbred: I never heard you say you did not.
Lady Wealthy: I'll say so now then, if you long.
Welbred: By no means. Say not a thing in haste you may
repent at leisure.
Lady Wealthy: Come, leave your fooling, or I'll swear it.
Welbred: Don't widow, for then you'll lie too.
Lady Wealthy: Indeed, it seems 'tis for my money you would have
me?
Welbred: For that, and something else you have.
Lady Wealthy: Well, I'll lay a wager thou hast lost all thy money in
play, for then you're allwaies in a marrying humour.
But, d'ye hear, gentleman, d'ye think to gain me
with this careless way, or that I will marry one I
don't think is in love with me?
Welbred: Why, I am.

Lady Wealthy: Then you would not be so merry. People in love are
　　　　　　　sad, and many times weep.
Welbred:　　　That will never do for thee, widow.
Lady Wealthy: And why?
Welbred:　　　'Twould argue me a child; and I am confident if
　　　　　　　thou didst not verily believe I were a man, I should
　　　　　　　ne'er be thy husband . . . weep for thee! ha! ha! ha!
　　　　　　　—if e'er I do!
Lady Wealthy: Go, hang yourself.
Welbred:　　　Thank you, for your advice.
Lady Wealthy: Well, then, shall I see you again?
Welbred:　　　When I have a mind to it. Come, I'll lead you to
　　　　　　　your coach for once.
Lady Wealthy: And I'll let you for once.[1]

(*Exeunt*)

Pepys saw this play on 8th December 1666 at 'The King's
House' and warmly praised Nell for her acting.

To the King's playhouse, and there did see a good part of *The
English Monsieur*, which is a mighty pretty play, very witty and
pleasant. And the women do very well, but, above all, little Nelly,
that I am mightily pleased with the play, and much with the
House, more than ever I expected, and very fine women.

In *The English Monsieur*, Nell has to speak these lines, which
well apply to her own life. "This life of mine can last no longer
than my beauty; and though 'tis pleasant now—I want nothing
whilst I am Mr. Wellbred's Mistress—yet, if his mind should
change, I might 'e'en sell oranges for my living; and he not buy
one of me to relieve me." How intrigued her audience would
have been to listen to these sentiments, aware that she and Hart
were lovers in real life.

It is a great pity that Nell Gwyn never acted in any of the plays
of Sir George Etherege, a far more skilful dramatist than James
Howard. How stimulating it would have been to see her in
the part of Belinda in *The Man of Mode* or *Sir Fopling Flutter*.
Etherege's comedies, however, were never performed at 'The
King's House'. He was too incorrigibly lazy to be a prolific
dramatist. *The Man of Mode* was first produced before the King at

'The Duke's House' in Dorset Garden on 11th March 1676 when Nell Gwyn had already left the stage.

The character of Dorimant, played by Thomas Betterton, is supposed to be modelled on that of John Wilmot second Earl of Rochester, an intimate friend of Etherege's. "I'll lay my life there's not an article but he has broken," says Pert in Act II, referring to "that base man Dorimant", who "talked to the vizards [masked ladies] i' the pit, waited upon the ladies from the boxes to their coaches, gone behind the scenes; and fawned upon those little insignificant creatures, the players. 'Tis impossible for a man of his inconstant temper to forebear, I'm sure." That might well be Rochester, or, perhaps, Buckhurst. Dorimant was an over-indulgent master to his servants, a celebrated fop, and a rake attractive to women. So was Rochester. But the second Duke of Dorset later claimed in conversation with Thomas Sheridan that the character of Dorimant was partly modelled on the remarkable wit, his grandfather, Charles Lord Buckhurst,[2] and partly on Lord Rochester. It is possible, however, that the dramatist was merely portraying himself, for Etherege was also renowned as a fop and seducer of women. Like Dorimant, we can easily imagine Etherege observing "How careful is nature in furnishing the world with necessary coxcombs!" The orange-woman in this play, who Dorimant describes as "that overgrown Jade with the Flasket of guts before her", is certainly unlike the attractive orange-wenches who sold their fruit in 'The King's House'.

The run of a play during the Restoration period was usually very short. Sometimes it would last for a few days, a week or even twelve days. On 20th December 1666 we find Nell Gwyn, as already mentioned, appearing in the important part of Celia in Beaumont and Fletcher's *The Humourous Lieutenant*. For the next six months Mrs. Ellen Gwyn was extremely busy, both rehearsing and performing in comedies.

On 23rd January 1667, Pepys visited 'The King's House', with his wife Elizabeth, to see *The Humourous Lieutenant*. It would seem that this work was a success, for it was still being performed at 'The King's House'. Pepys thought it a silly play, and he was no mean critic. Mrs. Mary Knipp, whose singing in this comedy pleased Pepys, was a colleague and friend of Nell Gwyn's for some years. As we know, Elizabeth Pepys was jealous of her husband's friendship with "that merry Jade" Knipp, though she would not have minded on this occasion being taken behind the scenes. "And Knipp took us all in," wrote the diarist, and we sense his excitement as he writes, "and brought to us Nelly, a most pretty woman, who acted the great part of Coelia today very fine, and did it pretty well." Pepys was especially delighted because of the opportunity to kiss Nelly, and his wife also embraced the young actress.

When Pepys, during February 1667, met Tom Killigrew at my Lord Brouncker's house, they discussed the theatre. Pepys was specially delighted when Killigrew confidentially told him that Mrs. Knipp was "Like to make the best actor that ever come upon the stage". They proposed to give her a rise of thirty pounds per annum. Unfortunately we do not know Mrs. Knipp's salary up to then. The Restoration players were certainly very poorly paid, and many of them were constantly in debt. Charles Hart, for instance, a leading actor at 'The King's House', only received about 146 pounds per annum.

Killigrew told Pepys that the many wax candles, now used in his theatre, were a great improvement on the three pounds of tallow candles formerly used. Tom Killigrew often visited Italy because he was an ardent lover of music, though he could not play a note. He was anxious to improve the standard of music in his theatre and to organize a concert for the King. For this purpose he intended to recruit the best Italian musicians.

Towards the end of February 1667, Nell Gwyn, aged only 17, created the important part of Florimel in John Dryden's new play, *Secret Love* or *The Maiden Queen*. Her acting in this delightful comedy was magnificent, and the rôle particularly suited to her genius. It was said that Dryden had especially written the part of Florimel for Nelly. Charles Hart played opposite her as the courtier Celadon, and the two were perfect foils for one another.

Most of us have visited a theatre to see some famous actress in a rôle in which she is superb. We have come away, as if still under the subtle spell of her enchantment, saying to ourselves, "I shall never see the like again. She *lived* the part." So was it with the spectators at 'The King's House', who crowded the pit and the

Nell Gwyn, by Simon Verelst, 1644–1710

Charles II, by Henri Gascar

galleries on that late February afternoon to see their Nelly play Florimel. The sauciness, the sensuality and the slight vulgarity of the character was ideal for her. Nelly, coming on to the stage in Act V dressed as a boy in breeches; saucy and irresistible when she discussed marriage with Charles Hart (Celadon). The enjoyment of the spectators was enhanced because they were aware that Hart and Nell were lovers in real life. After Nell Gwyn left the stage in 1671, *Secret Love* was revived at various periods. It was played before James II at Whitehall in December 1686, when William Mountfort took the part of Celadon created by Hart. It is not known who played Florimel, and we do not want to know.

This biographer admits to a craving to steal back in time 300 years or so ago to Restoration London, to be present at the first performance of *Secret Love*. There, in the pit on the backless benches, loll the gallants and fops, richly dressed and dallying with the orange-wenches, who are nothing loath to bandy words with them. Under the supervision of Orange Moll, the orange-wenches sell "the lovely fruit smiling with streaks of gold". There too, in the pit are seated the vizards (masked ladies), and many a curious glance is turned their way. 'Old Rowley'* is also there in a box, swarthy and saturnine, and by his side sits his adoring Portuguese-born queen, Catherine of Braganza, not slow, we can be sure, to show disapproval when the marriage vow is discussed too lightly during the play. For the first time Charles II is highly conscious of a certain talented actress named Mrs. Ellen Gwyn.

There was a strong cast. Beck Marshall (Mrs. Marshall) took the part of the Queen of Sicily; while Anne Quin, an actress who is sometimes confused with Nell Gwyn, was Candiope, a princess of the blood. Mrs. Knepp, or Knipp, was Asteria, the Queen's confidante; and Mrs. Cory, an original member of 'The King's House,' played Melissa. Little Major Mohun took the part of Philocles, the Queen's favourite, and Mr. Hart, as we have already said, was Celadon.

John Dryden tells us that *Secret Love* is based on a story in *The Cyrus*,[3] which he calls the Queen of Corinth, in whose character he portrays that of the celebrated Christian Alexandra,

* Charles II.

D

Queen of Sweden, daughter of Gustavus Adolphus II. Christina, destined to abdicate her throne, was born at Stockholm in 1626 and died at Rome in 1689, where she was given a magnificent funeral.

Was Dryden in fact describing Nell Gwyn when Celadon says:

A turn'd up nose, that gives an air to your face: Oh, I find I am more and more in love with you! a full neather-lip, an out-mouth, [Clifford Bax suggests this might signify 'a pouting mouth'], that makes mine water at it: the bottom of your cheeks, a little blub, and two dimples when you smile: for your stature 'tis well; and for your wit, 'twas given you by one that knew it had been thrown away upon an ill face: Come, you are handsome, there's no denying it.

Certainly some dialogue between Celadon and Florimel in Act II seems curiously prophetic of Nell's own life.

Celadon: But dost thou know what it is to be an old maid?

Florimel: No, nor I hope I shan't these twenty years.

Celadon: But when that time comes, in the first place thou wilt be condemn'd to tell stories how many men thou might'st have had: and none believe thee: Then thou growest froward, and impudently weariest all thy Friends to sollicite man for thee.

Florimel: Away with your old commonplace-wit: I am resolved to grow fat, and look young till forty, and then slip out of the world with the first wrinkle, and the reputation of five and twenty.

Nell never became either fat or hideous, but she did "slip out of the world" at the early age of 37, after some pain and an illness. She was throughout her life always excessively attractive to men, and there was never any need to 'sollicite' admirers.

Secret Love was a favourite play of Charles II's, and indeed he is supposed to have suggested the theme to Dryden. Charles, as Dryden himself informs us, "grac'd it with the Title of his play". It is, therefore, perhaps surprising, when we consider the King's character, that he expressed disapproval concerning the lax views regarding the married state which are taken in the play. It is likely, however, that Catherine of Braganza was shocked by the indelicacy of some of the passages, and she may have complained to her husband. All the same, the wit is scintillating, although the dialogue is certainly cynical. Prudish people would naturally object to it. Here is a lively passage from Act V:

> *Florimel:* But this marriage is such a Bugbear to me; much might be if we could invent by any way to make it easie.
>
> *Celadon:* Some foolish people have made it uneasie, by drawing the knot faster than they need; but we that are wiser will loosen it a little.
>
> *Florimel:* 'Tis true, indeed, there's some difference betwixt a girdle and an Halter.
>
> *Celadon:* As for the first year, according to the laudable custome of new married people, we shall follow one another up into Chambers, and down into gardens, and think we shall never have enough of one another—So far 'tis pleasant enough, I hope.
>
> *Florimel:* But after that, when we begin to live like husband and wife, and never come near one another—what then, Sir? . . .
>
> *Celadon:* When I have been at play, you shall never ask me what money I have lost.
>
> *Florimel:* When I have been abroad you shall never enquire who treated me.
>
> *Celadon:* Item, I will have the liberty to sleep all night, without your interrupting my repose for any evil design whatsoever.
>
> *Florimel:* Item, Then you shall bid me good night before you sleep.
>
> *Celadon:* Provided always, that whatever liberties we take with other people, we continue very honest to one another.
>
> *Florimel:* As far as will consist with a pleasant life.

A philosophy of marriage, which would certainly have appealed to the lascivious courtiers of Charles II's intimate circle. This celebrated scene between Florimel and Celadon is characteristic of the 'Proviso Scene', in which hero and heroine bargained about the conditions under which each might contemplate marriage.[4] Dryden's main source of strength as the writer of comedies was his pair of lovers.

Secret Love was a favourite play of Pepys, who saw it at least half a dozen times. He saw it first with his wife on 2nd March 1667 and confided to his diary:

> And the truth is, there is a comical part done by Nell, which is Florimell, that I never can hope ever to see the like done again, by man or woman. The King and Duke of York were at the play. But so great performance of a comical part was never, I believe, in the world before as Nell do this, both as a mad (madcap) girl, then most and best of all when she comes in like a young gallant; and hath the notions and carriage of a spark the most that ever I saw any man have. It makes me, I confess, admire her.

Together with Sir William Penn, Pepys was again present in the pit of the King's House on 25th May, all agog to see it once more, when he again praised Nell's acting. He also greatly admired Beck Marshall in the part of the Queen of Sicily. He could not see *The Maiden Queen* too often.

Beck Marshall was inclined to be hot-tempered. When Sir Hugh Middleton made some disparaging remarks about the actresses in the tiring-room of 'The King's House' one day in February 1667, Mrs. Marshall objected in no uncertain terms.[5] Sir Hugh became abusive and threatened to kill her, whereupon Beck complained to the King, who graciously promised her his protection. Sir Hugh, however, had her waylaid and attacked by a ruffian on her way home from the playhouse. Such incidents were not uncommon in the theatre. The courtiers thought of the actresses as little better than prostitutes and treated them as such.

Mrs. Ellen Gwyn made a striking success as Mirida, a madcap girl in the Honourable James Howard's delicious farce, *All Mistaken* or *The Mad Couple*, when it was produced at 'The King's House', probably for the first time, in April 1667. Charles Hart played opposite Nell as Philidor, a kinsman of an Italian duke; while John Lacy acted the part of Pinguister, a fat man, a rôle which would have suited him very well. In this play Nell is persecuted by two ridiculous lovers, a lean one and a fat one. The dialogue between Mirida and Pinguister must have been extremely diverting for the audience. It reminds one of the scene between Titania and Bottom.

Mirida:	Dear Love, come sit thee in my lap,
	and let me try if I can enclose thy
	world of fat and love within these arms.
	See I cannot nigh encompass my
	Desires by a mile.
Pinguister:	How is my fat a rival to my joys!
	Sure, I shall weep it all away.
Mirida:	Lie still, my babe, lie still and sleep,
(crooning)	It grieves me sore to see thee weep
	Wer't thou but leane, I were glad;
	Thy fatness makes thy dear love sad.
	What a lump of love have I in my arms!

One can imagine the pleasure and joy of the unsophisticated members of the audience at this stage, as they watched their Nelly, rolling farther and farther away from the fat man, whilst contriving so far as possible to show as much as possible of her shapely legs. Eventually she rose with a merry laugh, took two swords from a cutler and managed to disarm her fat suitor, a situation which endeared her even more to her many admirers. *All Mistaken* remained a favourite with Restoration audiences.

In the course of this play Nell Gwyn revealed her talents as a mimic, seemingly to make fun of a rival actress named Moll Davis of 'The Duke's House', who had recently enjoyed a remarkable success in *The Rivals*. It had been adapted by Sir William Davenant from an earlier play called *Two Noble Kinsmen* by Fletcher. Pretty Moll Davis, when acting Celania, a shepherdess mad for love, sang a song, whilst seated on the floor. The first verse went:

> My lodging it is on the cold ground,
>   And very hard is my fare,
> But that which troubles me most is,
>   The unkindness of my dear.
> Yet still I cry 'O turn love,
>   And I prythee, love, turn to me,
> For thou art the man that I long for
>   And alack, what remedy?'

So charming was little Mrs. Davis, fair and seductive as she pathetically sat on the bare boards, that she immediately captivated the susceptible heart of Charles II. According to Genest,

The Two Noble Kinsmen was acted as early as 1664. But Moll
Davis did not become a mistress of Charles II until January 1668.
She was no doubt furious when she heard that Nell Gwyn had
mimicked her in *All Mistaken* at 'The King's House'. Nell sang
(and how her audience must have responded to her naughtiness
and her clever miming of her rival):

> My lodging upon the cold floor is,
>   And wonderful hard is my fare,
> But that which troubles me more, is
>   The fatness of my dear.
> Yet still I cry 'O melt, love,
>   And I prythee now melt apace,
> For thou art the man I should long for
>   If 'twere not for thy grease.[5]'

By this time the spectators would be splitting their sides with
laughter, and some would be choking to restrain their tears as the
fat man Pinguister responded:

> Then prythee don't burden thy heart still,
>   And be deaf to my pitiful moan;
> Since I do endure the smart still,
>   And for my fat do groan.

Moll Davis was a superb dancer, and in that rôle she certainly
surpassed Nell Gwyn. Pepys was present at 'The Duke's Playhouse' on 7th November 1667 when Mrs. Davis appeared in *The
English Princesse* or *Richard III*, by J. Caryl, in Pepys' opinion
"a most sad, melancholy play, and pretty good . . . only little Miss
Davis did dance a jig at the end of the play, and there telling the
next day's play . . . and the truth is there is no comparison
between Nell's dancing the other day* and this, this being infinitely beyond the other". After she became Charles II's mistress,
Moll Davis on one occasion danced a jig before Queen Catherine
of Braganza at Whitehall, but the Queen hurriedly left the room.
Pepys relates that Moll was the natural daughter of Thomas
Howard, first Earl of Berkshire, which may account for her
inclination to put on airs. It is, however, just as likely that she was
the daughter of a blacksmith at Charlton in Wiltshire, where a

---

* As Florimel, in *Secret Love*, or *The Maiden Queen*.

family of the name of Davis had been established as blacksmiths for many years. Moll Davis made a striking success in *Sir Martin Marall*—a funny play, attributed to the Duke of Newcastle,* which Dryden certainly revised and adapted for the stage. When it was first performed in August 1667 at 'The Duke's House', Madame Davis took the part of Mrs. Millicent, a swashbuckler's daughter. If *Sir Martin Marall* or *The Feign'd Innocence* (as it was named) had been acted at 'The King's House', it is probable that Nell Gwyn would have played this part.

It is related that Charles Sackville Lord Buckhurst was so attracted by the spectacle of Nell rolling from side to side in *All Mistaken* and displaying a generous portion of her anatomy and her shapely legs, that he immediately decided to woo her for his mistress. Mrs. Gwyn, however, was very busy in the early part of 1667 as a leading actress in 'The King's House', playing as Flora in *Flora's Vagaries* by Rhodes, as Samira in Sir Robert Howard's *The Surprisal*, and possibly in other plays. According to Genest, though Dasent gives it a later date, Nell Gwyn and Charles Hart played the parts of Philaster and Bellario in *Philaster* or *Love Lies a Bleeding*, a tragedy by Beaumont and Fletcher, on 30th May 1667. A year later Pepys was present in 'The King's House' to see this play, but he does not mention Nelly. When it was revived in 1695, an actor named Horden, who spoke the prologue, said:

> For these bold parts we have no Hart, or Nelly,
> These darlings of the stage.

Among the rakes of the early Restoration period Charles Lord Buckhurst† (Nell's 'Charles II', for they were to have a brief liaison together) stands out pre-eminent. He was very handsome in his younger days, and a man obviously attractive to women. Despite his dissipated habits, as we have already said, Buckhurst was a man of wide culture, himself a witty poet and a munificent patron to men of letters. According to Clifford Bax, Buckhurst was the first to recognize the greatness of Milton's *Paradise Lost*. He was well known in his own time for the mordant wit of his

---

* *Sir Martin Marall*, originally a verse translation from the French, made by William, Duke of Newcastle.

† Born 1638, died 1708. Later sixth Earl of Dorset and Earl of Middlesex.

satires on contemporary personalities. Charles Sackville was son
of Richard fifth Earl of Dorset, and of Frances, daughter of Lionel
Cranfield, first Earl of Middlesex. Cranfield had been a shifty
politician in the reign of James I, but he certainly possessed a
shrewd financial brain.

Buckhurst is chiefly remembered today for his rollicking song,
'To all you ladies now at land', written, according to Matthew
Prior, when Buckhurst was serving as a volunteer in the fleet
against the Dutch during the First Dutch Wars in 1665. He
behaved with conspicuous gallantry, but it is far from certain that
he wrote these verses on this occasion. The first verse reads:

> To all you ladies now at land
> We men at sea indite;
> But first would have you understand
> How hard it is to write;
> The Muses now, and Neptune too,
> We must implore to write to you—
> With a fa, la, la, la, la.

Four years before he decided to seduce Nell Gwyn at 'The
King's House', my Lord Buckhurst, together with his intimate
friend Charles Sedley, also a member of "the merry gang", and
Sir Thomas Ogle,★ a knight of Pinchbeck, Lincolnshire, had been
involved in an extremely unsavoury affair. Having dined extremely well one summer day in June, the three friends "all
inflam'd with strong liquors", stripped themselves naked and
then appeared on the balcony of the Cock Tavern, naturally to
the horror of the many Puritans who were among the crowd
below.[6] After indulging in various revolting pranks, the drunken
Sir Charles preached a blasphemous sermon. He then proceeded
to imitate the gestures and antics of the itinerant quacks and
astrologers, who abounded in Restoration London, by recom-
mending "a powder as should make all the women of the town
run after him". By this time the people were growing greatly
incensed, and they began to fling stones at Sedley and his two
companions. As the chief offender, Sir Charles was summoned to
appear before Sir Robert Foster, Lord Chief Justice of the King's

★ Later in life a reformed character. Became Governor of Chelsea College.

Bench, who later ordered him to be fined 2,000 marks, imprisoned for a week without bail and bound over for good behaviour for three years. Buckhurst was also severely reprimanded. Five years later Pepys relates that Sedley and Buckhurst were discovered "running up and down all the night almost naked, through the streets and at last fighting, and being beat by the watch and clapped up all night".* This clearly shows that men capable of considerable achievement in creative literature behaved sometimes like irresponsible bounders.

Buckhurst, like Rochester, was in the habit of visiting the actresses in the tiring-rooms behind the scenes in 'The King's House'. He was a friend of Tom Killigrew, who would have made it easy for such a distinguished nobleman to penetrate wherever he wanted. Perhaps he had known Nell Gwyn whilst she was an orange-girl, though there is no proof of this. By the summer of 1667, gossips in the theatre were openly saying that she was Lord Buckhurst's mistress. No doubt Nell found her new lover attractive, though it is doubtful whether she really cared for him. Her colleagues in 'The King's House' envied her for having captivated a man of such distinction. He managed to retain the favour of Charles II throughout his reign. Buckhurst was certainly deeply experienced in the art of seducing girls, though Nell, with her essential honesty and frankness of manner, would have been willing to respond to Buckhurst's advances.

> None ever had so strange an art
> His passion to convey
> Into a list'ning virgin's heart,
> And steal her soul away.[7]

Nell, however, was already very experienced in sexual matters, while Buckhurst was almost 30. She was, during the summer of 1667, living in stuffy lodgings at 'The Cock and Pie' in Drury Lane. This tavern stood on the west side of Drury Lane, at its southern end and nearly opposite Wych Street. In Nell's day this street abounded with gabled and timbered Elizabethan houses. When Buckhurst suggested to her that they should go away for an unofficial honeymoon in Epsom, Nell showed considerable

* 23rd October 1668.

enthusiasm in accepting the proposition. What really amused her
was Buckhurst's intention to invite his intimate friend, Charles
Sedley, to be a member of the party. Nell then screwed up her
eyes in amusement, so that the dimples showed on her cheeks,
and her laughter was very merry. It is certain that Charles Hart
resented the loss of his mistress to Lord Buckhurst. He naturally
deplored her absence from the theatre, though the affair with this
nobleman was to be of a very temporary nature. On 13th July
1667, Pepys heard some news from Mr. Pierce which troubled
him: "That my Lord Buckhurst hath got Nell away from 'The
King's House', and gives her £100 a year, so as she hath sent her
parts to the house, and will act no more."

V   The Buckhurst Episode

PSOM was at this period a town of some beauty, a fashionable resort for those who wanted to drink the water. It so
happened that Samuel Pepys and a party of friends were
visiting Epsom on 14th July 1667, a lovely summer day. After
drinking four pints of the water, Pepys adjourned to 'The King's
Head', where he heard of the latest gossip concerning Nelly. He
wrote in his diary: "And to the towne, to the King's Head; and
hear that My Lord Buckhurst and Nelly are lodged at the next
house, and Sir Charles Sedley with them: and keep a merry house.
Poor girl! I pity her; but more the loss of her at the King's House."
Pepys was clearly not concerned overmuch with the moral issue,
for he was himself a libertine. What he really minded was the
temporary loss of Nelly from the stage, for he realized that the
affair with Buckhurst was unlikely to last.

Very few actresses after the Restoration led chaste lives. An
exception was Mrs. Sanderson, who later married Thomas Betterton, a great actor, particularly in tragedy. Nell Gwyn; Moll
Davis; Elizabeth Barry, a mistress of John Wilmot Earl of
Rochester and trained by him for the stage; and Margaret (Peg)
Hughes, a celebrated mistress of Prince Rupert, were all women of
immoral character. It is probable that the latter is the pretty
actress, named Pegg, who, according to Pepys, was formerly a
mistress of Sir Charles Sedley. Pepys kissed her on one occasion*
behind the scenes in 'The King's House'. Nell's friend, Mary
Knipp, seems to have divided her favours between Sir Charles
Sedley and Pepys. We know that her husband was a mean fellow,
"a kind of jockey", and that poor Knipp's life was far from happy,
owing to his surly and jealous moods.

* 8th May 1668.

The house in Epsom, where Nelly lived with Lord Buckhurst for a few brief weeks, must have echoed with sparkling and witty conversation. Local tradition maintains that it was a two-storied building with bow windows, which stood next to the King's Head Tavern. With her quick, nimble mind she would have been well able to cope with both her lover and Sedley. In the daytime, during these halcyon summer days, Buckhurst and Nelly would ride over the downs, only to dismount so as to enjoy the lovely views and the warm balmy air. And the gay suppers in the evenings, when Buckhurst and Sedley would argue over their wine in a stimulating manner about some new play, with Nelly's lively banter to encourage them. When night fell, Buckhurst was a tender, experienced lover, and the wildness, the feyness and the bizarre behaviour of Nelly enchanted the young nobleman for a while.

We may well wonder how Sedley passed the time when his friends were otherwise engaged, but he was very capable of looking after himself. On 5th August we know that he dined at 'The Durdans', Lord Berkeley's country home, near Epsom. A pious old lady, Mary Rich, Countess of Warwick, who was also dining that day at 'The Durdans', was much alarmed lest Sedley should misbehave. She wrote in her diary: "At dinner that day dined Sir Henry Sedley,* which was much trouble for me to see him lest he should be profane. But it pleased God to restrain him."¹ Sedley was firstly married to a Roman Catholic named Katherine Savage, who unfortunately held a fixed delusion that she was a queen and always insisted that she was to be addressed as 'Her Majesty'. Certainly Sir Charles's bouts of drinking at the Rose Tavern and his treatment of his unfortunate wife would not have helped her to recover her sanity. By this marriage Sedley had a daughter named Catherine, who subsequently became a notorious mistress of James Duke of York.

Despite his fondness for Sedley as a boon companion, Buckhurst seems later to have bitterly disliked Catherine Sedley, a coarse woman, who had inherited her father's wit. He later attacked her in his mordant satires, mocking her love of florid dresses and cosmetics.

* A mistake for Sir *Charles*.

> Tell me, Dorinda,* why so gay
> Why such Embroidery, Fringe and Lace
> Can any Dresser find a way
> To stop th' approaches of Decay
> And mend a Ruin'd Face!²

Another satire of Buckhurst's reads:

> Dorinda's sparkling witt and eyes
> United cast too fierce a light;
> Which blazes high, but quickly Dyes,
> Warms not the heart but hurts the sight.³

Some time in August Nell returned to London to take her original part of Cydaria in *The Indian Emperor*. Pepys, who disliked her in tragic parts, was critical of her acting. He wrote, on 22nd August:

> With my Lord Brouncker and his mistress to the King's playhouse, and there saw *The Indian Emperor*; where I find Nell come again, which I am glad of; but was most infinitely displeased with her being put to act the Emperor's daughter, which is a great and serious part, which she does most basely.

We do not exactly know what had happened, but it is evident that Nell and Lord Buckhurst had quarrelled. It is probable that she had pledged his credit in the Epsom shops, to buy jewellery or dresses, and that Buckhurst had told her that he would not be responsible for her purchases. He had already given her some money, and he was not prepared to continue to lavish her with presents. It may well be that Nell was longing to return to the stage, but she was loath for this pleasant association to cease. Yet it was not in keeping with her character to be lightly dismissed. She would give her protector a piece of her mind, and Buckhurst would be startled by her vehemence and her rich vocabulary of swear words. What is certain is that she returned to her career in London in a penurious condition. Nelly was never avaricious or grasping, but, like many artistic people, she had little sense of money. Buckhurst certainly lacked chivalry in ridding himself of a mistress who had given him a great deal of pleasure and amusement. Later in life, however, Buckhurst, after he had succeeded

* Dorinda was Catherine Sedley's nickname at Court.

as sixth Earl of Dorset, was one of Nell Gwyn's trustees when Charles II settled Burford House, Windsor, on her.[4] So it is evident that they remained pretty good friends, despite their broken liaison. Nell would refer to her former lover in a letter written to her intimate friend Laurence Hyde as "My lord Dorsett". Her letters were written for her by an amanuensis, for, as we have already seen, Nelly could not write herself.

On 26th August Orange Moll, all agog with the latest theatrical gossip, told Pepys and Sir William Penn

> that Nell is already left by my lord Buckhurst, and that he makes sport of her, and swears she hath had all she could get of him; and Hart, her great admirer, now hates her; and that she is very poor, and hath lost my Lady Castlemaine, who was her great friend also: but she is come to the House, but is neglected by them all.

Poor Nelly no doubt had to stomach the spiteful backchat of her colleagues, the sly innuendoes that my lord Buckhurst had tired of her very quickly. She had her pride, and she turned with scorn on Beck Marshall when that actress jibed at her. Hart had loved Nell Gwyn, and he now felt resentment when his former pupil, whom he had so skilfully trained for the stage, returned to 'The King's House'. It was said that Charles Hart now miscast Nell in tragic parts as a subtle form of revenge for her affair with My Lord Buckhurst. This does not, however, seem likely. What about that delightful comedy, *An Evening's Love* or *The Mock Astrologer*, produced on 12th June 1668, when she created the part of Donna Jacintha?

As for Lady Castlemaine, it is unlikely that she was ever Nell Gwyn's "great friend", for she was too busy having affairs with lithe young rope-dancers, like Jacob Hall of the Duke's Theatre, to have too much time for actresses. Possibly as a reprisal for Charles II's affair with Moll Davis, Lady Castlemaine, who was a nymphomaniac, took Jacob Hall to her bed during April 1668. Pepys always had a weakness for this malevolent woman, renowned for her beauty at Charles's court, with her auburn hair and voluptuous figure. Mrs. Knipp poured into his receptive ears on 7th April 1668 that "my Lady Castlemaine is mightily in love with Hall of their house (Duke of York's); and he is much with her in private, and she goes to him, and do give him many presents." Apparently Beck Marshall acted as the sole intermediary in their intrigue. On one occasion during February 1668, when the King gazed too ardently at Mrs. Davis, now his mistress, when he attended a play at the Duke's Theatre, Lady Castlemaine was "melancholy and out of humour, not smiling once". When she later became aware that Charles II was in love with Nell Gwyn, Lady Castlemaine retaliated by having a temporary liaison with Charles Hart.

Mrs. Ellen Gwyn, not yet 18, was very busy throughout the autumn of 1667, rehearsing and appearing in plays. She took the part of Panthea when Beaumont and Fletcher's *A King and no King* was revived in September. On 5th October she was playing Flora in *Flora's Vagaries* by Richard Rhodes and cursing very prettily because the pit was so badly attended. Mrs. Knipp, with whom Pepys was now becoming more infatuated, took him behind the scenes, gave him some fruit "and to the women's shift, where Nelly was dressing herself". He thought her "very pretty, prettier than I thought...." Pepys was shocked because so many depraved men visited the players behind the scenes. "But, Lord," he commented, ". . . and how lewdly they talk! and how poor the men are in clothes, and yet what a show they make on the stage by candle-light, is very observable." Mrs. Knipp's maid was so pretty that her mistress was afraid to keep her in her service, owing to the lecherous behaviour of the men.

It is possible, but by no means certain, that Mrs. Gwyn took the part of Alicia in Lord Orrery's tragedy, *The Black Prince*, which was presented at 'The King's House' on 19th October. Alice Perrers, the rapacious mistress of Edward III in his dotage, certainly resembled Barbara Villiers Countess of Castlemaine in character. It is more likely, however, that the part of Alicia was played by a leading actress of 'The King's House' named Anne Quin, who unfortunately has sometimes been confused with Nell Gwyn.

On 4th May 1667, the Lord Chamberlain ordered that Anne Quin should be given "a dressing roome with a chymney in it to be only for her use and whom she should admitt". Pepys saw *The Black Prince* for the first time on the afternoon of 19th October.

The play was apparently so popular that he could not find a seat in the pit and was compelled to pay four shillings for one of the upper boxes. If Nelly was in reality acting in this play, it is curious that Pepys does not mention her. When he was present on a later occasion, he thought it the worst of Lord Orrery's plays. He saw it for the last time on 1st April 1668, when he fell asleep in his box.

Nell Gwyn was given the important part of Donna Maria in Sir Robert Howard's *The Great Favourite* or *The Duke of Lerma*, presented on 20th February 1668. She spoke the prologue, together with Mrs. Knipp, and later the epilogue by herself. Pepys thought that Knipp had surpassed herself when speaking the prologue, "beyond any creature I ever heard. . . ." He may, however, have been prejudiced, for he was daily becoming more and more infatuated with her. The plot of *The Duke of Lerma* is concerned with the duke's attempt to prostitute his daughter to a king. In the prologue Nell and Knipp exchange some lively and malicious banter, which is certainly not of a high quality.

> *Knipp:* Deliver him from you that nothing spare,
> Nay, you that would fain seem worse than you are,
> Out-talk your own debaucheries and tell
> With a fine shrug, Faith, Jack I am not well.
> *Nell:* From you that with much ease, and little shame,
> Can blast a poet's, a woman's Fame,
> For at first sight a well-bred trick'y' have got,
> Combing your wiggs, to cry, Dam me, she's naught. . . .

Meanwhile, at the beginning of the new year (1668), Moll Davis had left 'The Duke's House' to become one of Charles II's mistresses. The King was at first much in love with her, gave her a ring worth 600 pounds and generously presented her with a richly furnished house in Suffolk Street. Mrs. Knipp, always well-informed about the latest gossip, told Pepys that King Charles had sent for Nelly several times. It would seem that Charles was now much attracted to Nelly and was considering her for a possible mistress.

Mrs. Davis had by the King one daughter named Lady Mary Tudor, who was later married to Francis second Earl of Derwentwater. Their son James Radclyffe, the third Earl, was to become

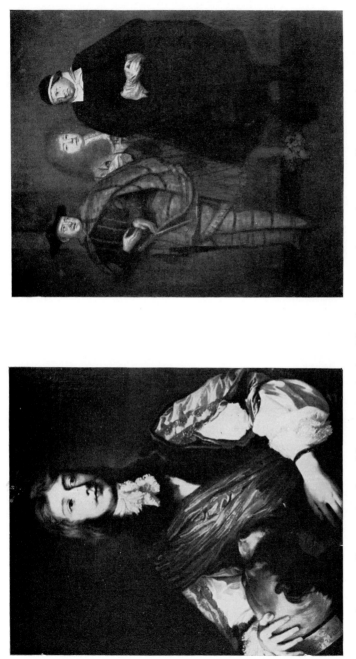

Thomas Killigrew. Attributed by Van Dyck. (*Right*) John Lacy in three roles as a gallant, a Presbyterian minister and a Highlander in his plaid. Painted by Michael Wright, probably in 1668–70

Nell Gwyn's horoscope, cast by Elias Ashmole

a loyal supporter of James III and to die nobly for the Jacobite cause in 1716.

We can conjecture that Nell Gwyn and Moll Davis never liked each other very much. Mrs. Davis, on her part, had never forgiven Nell for imitating her in *All Mistaken*. Nevertheless, being by nature very feminine and not being endowed with over-much intelligence, she was by no means reluctant to accept an invitation from her rival to a collation of sweetmeats. At the same time she would crow over Nell by showing her the magnificent ring her royal lover had given her. A sweet revenge, indeed, for fancied slights and real injuries. Meanwhile Nell had learnt—by what means we do not know—for even Mrs. Knipp was not omniscient, that Charles II intended to sleep with Moll Davis that night.*
With mischievous glee Nell then mixed the sweetmeats with jalap, a concoction which would have the effect of causing diarrhoea a few hours later. We can imagine the scene between Moll Davis and Nell Gwyn, Moll, ladylike and refined in manner and glancing with a possessive, proud look at her ring; while Nell was her usual flamboyant self and completely uninhibited. How eagerly Moll did justice to the sweetmeats, while Nell congratulated her on her good fortune in possessing such a ring. Later, however, when closeted with Charles II, Mrs. Davis would have needed a plentiful stock of oaths to curse Nelly, for that particular evening in the royal bed could not have been much of a success. Perhaps she was too refined to indulge in swearing. Anyhow, the capricious monarch soon tired of a mistress who had pretensions to be a lady. He was always so loath to part with any of the ladies of his harem, even if they were sometimes more troublesome than the spaniel bitches he loved to fondle. He gave Moll Davis a generous pension of 1,000 pounds a year, and she lived for some time in a house which was formerly number 22 in St. James's Square.† She really had few regrets in leaving the stage and no doubt would refer to her former colleagues in a superior manner when her friends could persuade her to talk about her days in 'The Duke's House'.

* The incident is related by Genest and other authors.
† Formerly part of the square, it was demolished in 1848 to make way for the Army and Navy Club.

E

A T the beginning of 1668 Nell Gwyn was a highly successful
actress, but she was still struggling to earn her living on
the stage. About now Nell made friends with a young
man named Villiers, who was distantly connected with George
Villiers second Duke of Buckingham and Barbara Villiers
Countess of Castlemaine. When Nell had a few hours to spare,
she liked to visit the rival playhouse, 'The Duke's House', and one
afternoon Villiers offered to escort her to the theatre. Whether
Villiers had designs on Nell we do not know, though it is certainly
likely. Anyhow he must have felt extremely uneasy when he discovered that King Charles II and his brother the Duke of York
were sitting near to them in an adjoining box. The King, who
was incognito, immediately started an animated conversation with
Nell Gwyn. Charles II was at once fascinated by Nell's complete
lack of affectation and by her natural behaviour, used as he undoubtedly was to the servility of the majority of the courtiers in
Whitehall. After the theatre the King suggested they should all
have supper together in a nearby tavern and that his brother might
come too, for the Duke of York could talk to Villiers, while he
could engage in some delightful sallies of wit with Nelly.

One cannot help feeling sorry for Villiers, uneasily aware of
the affinity between the affable King and the witty Nell. As he
listened to their laughter and banter he came to realize that there
was no chance of having a liaison with the young actress. He had
to listen while the Duke of York discussed various subjects. We
suspect that James described a fox hunt in which he had recently
taken part, or the state of the navy. As for Nelly, she was enjoying
herself enormously, especially when the tavern-keeper, who,
strange as it may seem, did not recognize the King, presented his

bill to the tall black man. Charles was hardly ever known to carry ready money on him, and it was not surprising when he eloquently shrugged his shoulders and said: "Odsfish! We have drunk too deep for my pocket,"* or some such expression, adding perhaps, "Come, James, you oblige." When appealed to, James possessed as little ready money as the King. Whereupon Nelly brilliantly imitated the King, as she said, mockingly: "Odsfish! but here is the poorest company that ever I was in at a tavern!" Poor Villiers had to pay for all four.

She knew that there was no risk that King Charles would be offended at her familiarity. The King desired her for his mistress, but for the present Nell was determined to remain on the stage, and we can be grateful for her decision. No doubt the King sent for Nelly several times after this chance encounter, and Nelly was more than willing to grant him her favours.

When *The English Monsieur* was revived during March and April 1668, Nell played her old part of Lady Wealthy. She also appeared as Lucilla in *The Man's the Master* when it was presented in early May. Sir William Davenant, who had recently died, had translated this play from the French. Pepys had no high opinion of it when he saw it at the Duke of York's House on 26th March. "Most of the mirth was sorry, poor stuffe, of eating of sack posset and slabbering themselves and mirth fit for clownes," he wrote. It would seem that Tom Killigrew was later able to present *The Man's the Master* at 'The King's House'. Nell then wore boy's clothes and looked very becoming.

It is probable, but by no means certain, that Nell played the part of Victoria, a madcap character, in Sir Charles Sedley's play *The Mulberry Garden* when it was produced at 'The King's House'. The first performance, on 18th May 1668, was a splendid occasion. Both King Charles and Queen Catherine of Braganza were present, and all Sedley's friends were there, in large flaxen periwigs and elegant suits, among them Etherege, Rochester, Henry Savile† and the Duke of Buckingham. Pepys too was there, having first dined off half a breast of mutton at the Rose Tavern. He was, however, disappointed in the play, and in his usual

* Clifford Bax suggests that the King said this.
† A brother of Edward Savile, later Marquis of Halifax.

observant way noticed that the King neither laughed nor seemed pleased with it from the beginning to the end. It is curious that Pepys disliked it, for earlier that month he had accompanied Mrs. Knipp to her lodgings, when she was being taught one of the songs in Act III of *The Mulberry Garden* by a musician named Bannister. In January she had referred to Sir Charles Sedley's *The Wandering Ladys*, but it is not known by that name. Despite its somewhat frigid reception on 18th May, *The Mulberry Garden* was subsequently a success. Many years later, on 23rd May 1687, Sir George Etherege, writing from Ratisbon where he was temporarily employed as a diplomat, mentions Sedley's comedy *Bellamira* and refers to *The Mulberry Garden*. "Some barren sparks have found fault with what he has formerly done on this occasion, onely because the fatness of the soile has produc'd too big a crop."[1] The play took its name from a mulberry garden or a plantation of mulberry trees on the site where Buckingham Palace now stands, laid out by King James I. Pepys found it a very silly place, "worse than Spring-Garden", and but little company, "only a wilderness here, that is somewhat pretty."

Sedley in his younger days was certainly extremely unstable and a debauchee, but capable of writing poignant lyrical poetry of a rare loveliness, such as the following lines in a poem named 'Constancy':

> Fear not my Dear, a flame can never die,
> That is once kindled by so bright an eye, . . .
> For though thy beauty first assured my sight,
> Yet now I look on it but as the light
> That led me to the Treasury of thy mind.

On Friday, 12th June 1668, Mrs. Ellen Gwyn created the part of Donna Jacintha in John Dryden's new comedy, *An Evening's Love*[2] or *The Mock Astrologer*, while Charles Hart played opposite her as Wildblood, a rôle in which he excelled. Major Mohun took the part of Bellamy, a young English gentleman in Madrid; and Mrs. Knipp had the congenial part of Beatrix, a confidante of the two noble Spanish ladies. *An Evening's Love* abounds in humour, wit and gaiety, though Donna Jacintha and Wildblood are possibly not such skilfully drawn characters as Florimel and Celadon in *Secret Love*. Charles II and Catherine of Braganza were probably at the Theatre Royal that afternoon.

The source of Dryden's play is originally taken from Calderon's *El Astrologio Fingido*, as he informs us in his preface. The critic, Gerard Langbaine, who detested Dryden, suggested that *An Evening's Love* has "little Hints borrow'd from Shakespeare, Petronius Arbiter, and other authors", and he constantly accused Dryden of plagiarism. He dedicated his comedy to William Duke of Newcastle, a wonderful horseman.

Pepys relates, on 19th June: "My wife and Deb (their maid) have been at the King's playhouse today, thinking to spy me there; and saw the new play *Evening Love* of Dryden's. . . ." Mrs. Pepys told her husband that she did not care for the play. It is fair to say that Mrs. Pepys was indulging "a melancholy, fusty humour" on that day, which may account for her opinion of *Evening Love*. When Pepys visited 'The King's House' on the following afternoon he was unfavourably impressed. He was not always a discerning critic. He found it "very smutty, and nothing so good as *The Maiden Queen* or *The Indian Emperor*". Is it possible that the text, first published in 1671, was amended from the original version? To read *An Evening's Love* is a delight, and there is certainly nothing smutty in it. Evelyn too, a censorious critic, who, unlike Pepys, did not particularly care for the theatre, wrote in his diary:[3] "To a new play with several of my relations, *The Evening Lover*, a foolish plot, and very prophane; it afflicted me to see how the stage was degenerated and polluted by ye licentious times."

We can imagine that the gay and lively part of Donna Jacintha suited Nell Gwyn, though her best rôle in Dryden's comedies will always remain the irresistible Florimel. Madrid at Carnival time was certainly an agreeable setting for the witty dialogue between Wildblood and Donna Jacintha.

Here is some dialogue between Donna Jacintha (Nell) and her confidante Beatrix (Mrs. Knipp):

Beatrix: You do love him (Wildblood) then?
Jacintha: Yes, most vehemently.
Beatrix: But set some bounds to your affection.
Jacintha: None but fools confine their pleasure: what insurer ever thought his coffers held too much? No, I'll give myself the swinge, and love without reserve. If I'll keep a passion, I'll never starve it in my service.

Nell too, in her own life, was to love without reserve and with a generosity few women are capable of. Yet there was a brazen, worldly quality in Jacintha. How well Dryden had studied the women in that hard, brittle society of the Restoration period, not altogether unlike our own. When Wildblood asks Jacintha "Then what is a gentleman to hope from you?" Jacintha replies—and for the audience the message must have been very revealing—"To be admitted to pass my time with, while a better comes; to be the lowest step in my staircase, for a knight to mount upon him, and a Lord upon him, and a marquess upon him, and a duke upon him, till I get as high as I can climb."* Dryden might well have added "a King to climb upon a Duke", but he would hardly have dared to, especially as King Charles was present at the first performance. Wildblood compares Jacintha to "the women of the playhouse, still piquing at each other, who shall go the best drest, and in the richest habits: till you work up one another by your high flying, as the heron and falcon do. . . ." This play has an asperity, a bitterness, which is lacking in *Secret Love*.

Dryden's gifts were as a satirist, rather than as a lyric poet. All the same he wrote some charming songs for *An Evening's Love*. One in Act V is really a duet between Damon (Charles Hart) and Celimena (Nell Gwyn). Here are three verses:

> *Damon:*   Celimena of my heart
> None shall e're bereave you:
> If with your good leave I may
> Quarrel with you once a day,
> I will never leave you.
>
> *Celimena:* Passion's but an empty name
> Where respect is wanting:
> Damon you mistake your ayme;
> Hang your heart, and burn your flame,
> If you must be ranting.
>
> *Damon:*   Love as dull and muddy is,
> As decaying liquor:
> Anger sets it on the lees,
> And refines it by degrees,
> Till it works the quicker.

* Act IV.

Mrs. Ellen Gwyn spoke the epilogue, and Dryden used her as a mouthpiece to attack the critics, who were particularly venomous during that age:

> My part being small, I have had time today,
> To mark your various censures of our Play:
> First, looking for a judgement or a wit,
> Like Jews I saw 'em scatter'd through the Pit:
> And where a knot of smilers lent an eare
> To one that talk'd, I knew the foe was there.
> The club of jests went round; he who had none
> Borrow'd o' th' next, and told it for his own:
> Among the rest they kept a fearfull stir,
> And said, betwixte a French and English Plot
> He eas'd his half-tir'd Muse, on pace and trot.
> Up starts a Monsieur new come o're; and warm
> In the French stoop; and the pull-back o' th' arm;
> Morbleu, dit-il, and cocks, I am a rogue
> But he has quite spoil'd the feint Astrologue.

The coarse-minded audience would revel in the jibes at the French as foreigners. The favourite part of the theatre for the critic was known as Fop Corner, where the fashionable courtiers and the snarling critics crowded, often to sneer at a play.

After Nelly left the stage in 1671, *An Evening's Love* was still acted for many years. On two occasions during 1686 it was played before James II and his Italian-born queen, Mary of Modena, at Whitehall.

Pepys constantly gives us many little touches revealing Nelly. When he was present in an upper box with his wife on 7th January 1669 to see *The Island Princess*, a tragi-comedy by Beaumont and Fletcher, there she was in the next box: "A bold merry slut who lay laughing there upon people". A friend from 'The Duke's House' was with her. It seems clear that Nelly, who was always completely natural, wanted the people to share her pleasure that she was now the King's mistress.

There were many, however, who strongly disapproved of Charles II's immorality and low taste for actresses. A typical example was the M.P. for Weymouth, Sir John Coventry, who proposed during 1669 in the House of Commons that a tax should

be levied on the playhouses. This motion was objected to by
Sir John Birkenhead, a friend of the King's, who maintained that
the players were the King's servants and a part of his pleasure.[4]
Sir John then pointedly asked, whether His Majesty's pleasure lay
among the men or the women that acted. According to Genest,[5]
the King was now determined to take a severe revenge. This is
indeed highly improbable, because Charles II was seldom vindic-
tive. As Coventry was returning to his home in Suffolk Street one
night, he was waylaid and attacked by some ruffians. One of the
ringleaders was a lieutenant in the Duke of Monmouth's troop of
guards. It seems likely therefore that the King's natural son was the
real instigator of this affair. Coventry bravely defended himself,
but his nose was slit to the bone, and he was gravely wounded.
The ringleaders were eventually banished for their part in this
assault.

By the beginning of January, 1669, Pepys felt obliged to confess
that his relationship with Mrs. Knipp had reached a difficult pass.
He was faced with the predicament of any unfaithful husband who
has to submit to the taunts of a jealous wife. When, together with
his wife, he saw *Secret Love* for the last time, Pepys was embarrassed when "Knepp looked upon us, but I durst not shew her any
countenance, and, as well as I could carry myself, I found my wife
uneasy there, poor wretch! . . ." He would avoid going to 'The
King's House' as much as possible in the future. Mrs. Mary Knipp
was arrested on several occasions; for instance on 23rd April 1668,
she is referred to as "one of ye comedians of Ye Royall Theatre"
and taken into custody for various misdemeanours there. When
Ben Johnson's old play *Cataline's Conspiracy* was played at 'The
King's House' on 19th December 1668, Mrs. Ellen Gwyn and
Mrs. Mary Knipp both spoke the prologue. Nell Gwyn wore an
Amazonian habit in this play, but was not given any definite
part.

Nell on one occasion in October 1668 played the part of a
guardian angel named Angelo in *The Virgin Martyr* by Massinger
and Dekker. Pepys had gone backstage to fetch his lady friend,
Mrs. Knipp, just as Beck Marshall, looking "mighty fine and
pretty and noble" in a white robe and wearing a crown, came off
the stage. Nell was there too, dressed as a boy. "But, Lord!" com-

mented the diarist, "Their confidence! and how many men do hover about them as soon as they come off the stage, and how confident [impudent] they are in their talk!"

Her most important part during 1669 was as Valeria in John Dryden's new tragedy, *Tyrannick Love, or The Royal Martyr.* The first performance occurred during the last week of June, and it achieved a notable success. The King, in a most affable mood, congratulated his crony Tom Killigrew, and said that he was vastly pleased. It was played for two consecutive weeks—a long run for a Restoration play. The cast was a distinguished one.

Major Mohun acted the part of the tyrant Maximin, father of Valeria, while Charles Hart played Porphyrius. Edward Kynaston, a very fine actor with a handsome presence, was given the rôle of Placidius. Cibber relates that, when scarcely a boy, Kynaston was a great favourite of the fashionable ladies, who liked to drive him round the 'tour' of Hyde Park in his stage clothes. He had "a piercing eye and in characters of heroick life a Quick imperious vivacity in his tone of voice that painted the tyrant truly terrible".[6] Ted Kynaston bore a striking resemblance to Sir Charles Sedley, which was unfortunate. He was rash enough, whilst appearing in a play called *Heiress*, to array himself in clothes that resembled those of Sir Charles and to ridicule the baronet. Some months before *Tyrannick Love* was presented on the stage, Kynaston, very unwisely, took a walk in St. James's Park wearing the laced clothes in which he had impersonated Sedley on the stage. As a gentleman, Sedley could not tolerate such insolence from a mere actor. He ordered two ruffians to attack the actor in the park, a form of revenge often resorted to in that age of violence. Kynaston was so bruised that he was obliged to take to his bed, whilst an understudy read his part on the stage.

If Nell Gwyn was as poor in tragedy as has been alleged, it is curious that Killigrew cast her in such parts. She certainly gave a striking performance in the part of Valeria, though she genuinely disliked appearing in serious plays. The other female rôles were taken by Mrs. Marshall, who played Berenice, Maximin's wife; and by Mrs. Hughes, who played St. Catharine. It is not clear whether the 'Mrs. Marshall' referred to is Beck (Rebecca) or Ann.

It is probable that Mrs. Hughes is the Peg Hughes, who subsequently became Prince Rupert of the Rhine's mistress and presented him with a daughter named Ruperta. Nell Gwyn's friend, Mrs. Mary Knipp, doubled Felicia and the aetherial spirit, Nakar. Mrs. Susanna Uphill, the beautiful but imperious mistress of Sir Robert Howard, had the small part of Erotian.

Legal disputes frequently occurred in the Restoration playhouse, and *Tyrannick Love* resulted in a Chancery action brought by Killigrew, Hart and Mohun against a scenic painter called Isaac Fuller. They alleged that he had not completed "the painting of the scenes" within the specified time. Fuller, however, eventually succeeded in winning his case against Killigrew and his colleagues in the Court of Exchequer. The painter was awarded 335 pounds ·10 shillings—the value of the work.[7]

When dedicating this play to James, Duke of Monmouth, Dryden reminded him that he had dedicated an earlier play, *The Indian Emperor*, to his wife Anna, Duchess of Monmouth.

There is little doubt that Dryden was keenly interested in the occult and the metaphysical. Yet he tells us in his preface:

As for what I have said of astral or aerial spirits, it is no invention of mine, but taken from those who have written on that subject. Whether there are such Beings or not, it concerns not me: 'Tis sufficient for my purpose, that many have believ'd the affirmative: and that these Heroick Representations, which are of the same Nature with the Epick, are not limited, but with the extremest bounds of what is credible.

In this play Mrs. Ellen Gwyn, a Roman princess, is compelled to stab herself in the last scene. Let us imagine the frantic despair of the spectators in 'The King's House', for they loved Nelly as their own and could not bear to see her carried off the stage. Then their spontaneous joy as she suddenly leapt to life, giving one of the bearers a smart box on the ears, and cried:

Hold! Are you mad, you damn'd confounded dog!
I am to rise and speak the epilogue!'

Then, taking the audience into her confidence:

I come, kind gentlemen, strange news to tell ye,
I am the ghost of poor departed Nelly.
Sweet ladies, be not frightened, I'll be civil,
I'm what I was, a little harmless Devil.
For, after Death, we sprights have just such Natures,
We had for all the world, when humane Creatures;
And therefore I that was an actress here,
Play all my Tricks in Hell, a goblin there.
Gallant's look to 't, you say there are no sprights,
But I'll come dance about your Beds at nights.

Then she is Puck, chuckling and confiding in her audience.

And 'faith you'll be in a sweet kind of taking,
When I surprise you between sleep and waking.
To tell you true, I walk because I dye
Out of my calling in a Tragedy.
O poet! damn'd dull poet, who could prove
So senseless, to make Nelly dye for love,
Nay, what's yet worse, to kill me in the prime
Of Easter-Term, in Tart and Cheese-cake time!

Then the last two lines of Dryden's epilogue:

Here Nelly lies, who, though she liv'd a slatern'n
Yet dyed a Princess acting in St. Cathar'n.

For the first time we have a sense of loss that Pepys, already haunted by the thought of approaching blindness, was not there on that June afternoon to record his impressions.

It was said that King Charles was so enchanted with Nelly's performance as Valeria that he bore her away to supper and later to his bed in Whitehall. We know that by August 1669 Nell Gwyn was *enceinte*. For some months she was absent altogether from the stage.

Nelly's 'Charles the Third'

THE time is now ripe to discuss the love life of Charles II. We are not really concerned with the political aspects of his complex character—a consummate master of kingcraft as he is generally acknowledged to be today. Nell Gwyn, unlike her rival, Louise de Kéroualle, later Duchess of Portsmouth, very rarely interfered in political matters. She was perfectly content to be a "sleeping partner in the ship of State", as she referred to herself.

Charles II was at least six feet tall, possessed a good figure, and his voice was very deep. His face was saturnine and harsh, but he was of a merry, affable disposition. His eyes were dark and brilliant, and his face swarthy. Yet there was a melancholy trait in his character, which has never been sufficiently stressed. That is one reason why Nell retained her position at Court for longer than most of her rivals. By her gaiety and spontaneous wit she made herself indispensable to the King, who needed to be constantly amused.

In Charles's veins flowed the warm, sensual blood of his maternal grandfather, Henri Quatre. His swarthiness and apparent indolence may have been owing to a Moorish strain in the Medici family, for his maternal grandmother was Marie de Medici. Throughout his life he possessed so many mistresses that it is difficult to account for them all. During his life in exile the two most important were Lucy Walter, a Welshwoman, the mother of the Duke of Monmouth, "a browne, beautiful, bold but insipid creature", as she has been described;* and Catherine Pegge, the daughter of a Derbyshire squire. Catherine Pegge was also a beauty, and, whilst Charles was in exile in Bruges during 1657,

---

* By John Evelyn, 18th August 1649.

she presented him with a son. Nell Gwyn was then a mere child of 7, running wild in the streets round Drury Lane. After the Restoration the King created this son Earl of Plymouth, but he was known as Don Carlo at Court.

One of the secrets of Nell Gwyn's hold over Charles II was that she appealed strongly to the bohemian side of his character. Charles, as is well known, was one of the most affable kings who ever sat on the throne of England. Although he could be dignified if he chose, he really hated ceremony and constraint. He loved to saunter in the park, and chat familiarly with his subjects. He was most at ease at Newmarket, where he could sup and bandy wit with the jockeys.

On the other hand, Louise de Kéroualle appealed to the intellectual and artistic side of his character; while Barbara Villiers, Countess of Castlemaine, dominated Charles for some years at the beginning of his reign because he was infatuated with her physical beauty. When she became a Catholic, though nobody believed her conversion to be genuine, Charles remarked that he never interfered with the souls of his ladies.

How many of his mistresses really loved Charles II? Barbara Villiers, as we have seen, was unfaithful to him; while Louise de Kéroualle, a calculating minx, cared for the King so long as he loaded her with presents and jewellery. The lovely Frances Stuart, later Duchess of Richmond, almost certainly never became his mistress, although the King was passionately in love with her in 1664 and 1665.

Catherine of Braganza, Charles II's Portuguese-born Queen, certainly adored her husband and, in characteristic Latin fashion, was extremely jealous of his mistresses. She particularly detested Lady Castlemaine, whom Charles had insisted on creating a lady of her bedchamber. Later Catherine was compelled to reconcile herself to the fact that mistresses were essential to a man of Charles's peculiar temperament. In any case kings were expected to have them in those days. Although she was sometimes jealous of Louise de Kéroualle, Duchess of Portsmouth, she was obliged to accept the situation. Her own influence on her capricious husband was by no means negligible, and Charles later became devoted to her as a companion. Catherine of Braganza never

seems to have resented Nell Gwyn and indeed preferred her to her
rival, Louise de Kéroualle. If she disliked the young actress, it is
difficult to understand her apparent fondness for Nell's elder son
by Charles II, Charles Duke of St. Albans. We know that, after
Charles II's death, his widowed queen gave him a pension.

Bishop Gilbert Burnet refers to Nell Gwyn as "the indiscreetest
and wildest creature that ever was in a Court".[1] It was indeed
what have been described as Nell's "buoyant indiscretions" which
enchanted Charles II. Rochester tells us in his 'Panegyric on Nelly':

> There's Hart's and Rowley's soul she did insnare,
> and made a King a rival to a player.

He was already about 39 when Nell became his mistress, while
she was 19. If Bishop Burnet is to be believed, the Duke of Buckingham told him, four years after Nell Gwyn had become the
King's mistress, that she had asked only 500 pounds a year from
her royal lover—hardly an indication of a grasping nature. Later,
according to Burnet, the King had given her over 60,000 pounds.[2]
Jesse relates that she had not a grain of avarice in her nature.
Burnet, with gross ill-taste and with a lack of candour and truth,
alleges that the King "never treated her with the decencies of a
mistress, but rather with the lewdness of a prostitute, as she had
been indeed to a great many; and therefore she called the King
her Charles the Third, since she has been formerly kept by two of
that name" (Charles Hart and Charles Lord Buckhurst). The
definition of a prostitute is a woman who offers her body to indis-
criminate sexual intercourse for money. Nell was not a natural
wanton, and Burnet erred in calling her a prostitute. She certainly
loved "her Charles the Third", was grateful for his generosity and
was faithful to him for the rest of his life. Charles II himself told
Burnet on one occasion that "God would not damn a man for a
little irregular pleasure out of the way". On the whole he was as
attached to his dogs as he was to some of his mistresses, allowing
them to lie in his bed-chamber to pup and give suck. All the same,
the Venetian diplomat Pietro Mocenigo was shrewd enough to
perceive in 1671, when Charles II was 41, that his pleasures did
not distract his attention from concerning himself with the serious
affairs of the country.

George Savile,[3] later Marquess of Halifax, relates that it was resolved by others whom Charles II should have in his arms, as well as whom he should have in his councils. This statement certainly bears the stamp of truth, for that shrewd statesman knew the King very well. The King, however, chose Nell for her own qualities and because he was genuinely in love with her. Savile observed: "His mistresses were as different in their humours as they were in their looks." James Welwood[4] tells us that "Charles II was a great votary to love, and yet the easiest and most uncloncern'd Rival. He was for the most part not very nice in the choice of his mistresses, and seldom possess'd of their first favours, yet would sacrifice all to please them". Yet he tormented himself with jealousy when Frances Stuart, who had always eluded him, eloped with the Duke of Richmond. He resented it when any of the courtiers made advances to Nelly.

In 1668 an important new appointment was made in the royal household. William Chiffinch succeeded his brother Thomas as page of His Majesty's bedchamber and Keeper of the King's private closet. Nell got to know him well, and later in her career would often sup, together with her friends, in his apartments. What stories could this confidential pander to the King's desires have revealed, if only he had written his memoirs, of the sly, unknown mistresses who had been escorted up the back stairs in the Palace of Whitehall, dark and silent at night, to the King's bedchamber to satisfy for a brief hour or so the sexual appetite of his master. As David Ogg rightly says: "Chiffinch performed a great and honourable service to the Stuarts by not writing his memoirs."[5] Will Chiffinch acted as confidential agent, and pawn-broker-in-chief to the King, and he was so well-informed concerning the reputation of Charles II's courtiers that he could have blackmailed most of them if he had so chosen. Pepys was acquainted with him and would sometimes dine with him on pickled herring.

William Chiffinch, who delighted in political intrigues as well as amorous ones, was an invaluable servant to such a master as Charles II. He often acted as spy and informer, enticing men to become drunk so that he could wheedle information from them. But he usually remained sober himself, for he made use of a

powerful restorative invented by a Dr. Goddard and known as
'Dr. Goddard's Drops', or 'The King's Drops'. For showing ladies
of easy virtue up the back stairs to the King's assignation rooms,
Madame Chiffinch was rewarded with 1,200 pounds per annum.

Nelly and her royal lover were both extremely witty and vied
with each other in this respect. On one occasion, when the King
was attending a theatre, he remarked upon the grim looks of the
murderers in *Macbeth*. "Pray, what is the reason that we never see
a rogue in a play, but, odsfish!, they always clap him on a black
periwig, when it is well known one of the greatest rogues in
England always wears a fair one?" It is almost certain that he was
referring to Anthony Ashley Cooper Earl of Shaftesbury,*
renowned for his insolent wit. Charles II once called him, as Lord
Chancellor, "the greatest rogue in England". Shaftesbury retorted
"Of a subject, Sir, perhaps I am." After Charles had been shown
his portrait by Riley, the artist, he observed: "Is that like me?—
then, odsfish!, I am an ugly fellow." He was usually courteous and
knew how to administer a gentle rebuke. Once, when William
Penn, the Quaker and future founder of Pennsylvania visited the
King, he kept on his hat according to the custom of his sect. Penn
expressed surprise when the King took off his hat, saying: "Friend
Charles, why dost thou not keep on thy hat?" " 'Tis the custom
of this place that only one person should be covered at a time,"
replied Charles.

John Wilmot Earl of Rochester's epitaph on Charles II is well
known, but bears repetition:

> Here lies a great and mighty king,
> Whose promise none relies on.
> He never said a Foolish thing,
> Nor ever did a wise one.

Charles made a characteristic retort. "The matter is easily
accounted for; my discourse is my own, while my actions are my
ministers." The Duke of Buckingham once referred to King
Charles II "as the father of his people", and, *sotto voce*, he added,
"of a good many of them." On 8th May 1670 Nell Gwyn gave

---

* It is just possible he was referring to Titus Oates.

birth to a son, who was christened Charles after his father. Anthony à Wood, the antiquary of Oxford, wrote in his diary on 12th May: "Elianor Quin, one that belongs to the King's Playhouse, was brought to bed of a boy in her house in Lincoln's Inn Fields, next to Whetstone Park—the King's bastard."[6] The King would often visit his new mistress there.

Meanwhile John Dryden, who had been created poet laureate in 1670, had written a new play called *Almanzor and Almahide* or *The Conquest of Granada.* He had originally intended it to be presented in the spring (1670), but, owing to the pregnancy of Nell Gwyn, this was not possible. Both Dryden and Tom Killigrew were keen that Mrs. Ellen Gwyn should be given the part of Almahide, Queen of Granada, and that she should speak the epilogue in the first part of the play. This tragedy is one of the finest works of Dryden, though Gerard Langbaine attacked the dramatist for being "so pufft up with vanity".[7] He makes his customary accusation of plagiarism; that Dryden had introduced into the drama the characters of Ferdinand and Isabella and the Duke of Arcos, though it is difficult to understand how a play about the fall of Granada could fail to include these historical personalities. The dramatist himself admits in the preface to *An Evening's Love*: "Whenever I have Lik'd any story in a Romance, Novel or foreign play, I have made no difficulty, nor ever shall, to take the foundation of it, to build it up, and to make it proper for the English Stage." Certainly Dryden borrowed several incidents from Mlle de Scudery's romance, *Almihide* or *L'Esclave Reine.*

It is likely that, during May 1670, Charles II was thinking of his sister Henrietta rather than of his mistress at Lincoln's Inn Fields. There then occurred an historical event, which was later to influence the presentation of *The Conquest of Granada* in the autumn. Henrietta, Duchess of Orleans, youngest sister of Charles II, the beloved 'Minette', one of the few people whom Charles ever really loved, came to Dover to visit her brother. She was accompanied by a suite of 237 persons, including her demure and extremely pretty maid-of-honour, Louise de Kéroualle, the daughter of a noble but impoverished Breton family. The purpose

F

of this visit was mainly political, to complete the final negotiations for framing the Secret Treaty of Dover, 'The *Traité de Madame*', as it is sometimes called. In return for an annual subsidy of 2,000,000 livres from King Louis XIV of France, Charles II was to make a perpetual alliance between England and France.

The latest French fashions in dress among Henrietta's retinue caused amusement and ridicule among the English. The French ladies sported enormous circular hats, known as 'cartwheels' by the English; while the gentlemen wore extremely short coats with broad waist-belts. During Madame's visit, the company of 'The Duke of York's House', including their brilliant comedian James Nokes, had visited Canterbury, where they had performed two comedies and a ballet before Charles II and his sister. The plays were Shadwell's *Sullen Lovers* and Caryl's *Sir Solomon* or *The Cautious Coxcomb*. To ridicule the French, which was very bad manners, Nokes wore an extremely short-laced scarlet coat with a broad waist-belt when playing the part of Sir Arthur Addle, a noted fop. The Duke of Monmouth gave the actor his own sword, which Nokes proudly retained for the rest of his life.

The susceptible King was immediately attracted during Henrietta's visit by "the baby-faced Bretonne", Louise* de Kéroualle, who attended her. Madame was anxious to give her brother a jewel as a return for the lavish presents he had loaded her with. She therefore ordered Louise to bring her jewel-casket, so that her brother might choose for himself. Charles then took the blushing maid-of-honour by the hand and ardently declared that she was the only jewel he coveted. No doubt aware of her brother's temperament, Henrietta sensibly declined to leave the girl in England, telling him that she was responsible for the girl's safety and had promised her parents to bring her back to France. Louise de Kéroualle later became Nell Gwyn's detested rival at Court.

With gross ill taste, the management of the Duke's Theatre exploited the situation by allowing James Nokes to appear on the stage in an absurd short coat, designed to ridicule the French. So comic was James Nokes, that he had only to appear on any stage to be greeted by howls of laughter. According to Colley Cibber,[8]

* Her full names were Louise Renée de Penancoet.

He was an actor of a quite different genius from any I have ever read, heard of, or seen, since or before his time; and yet his general excellence may be comprehended in one article, namely a plain and palpable simplicity of nature, which was so utterly his own, that he was often as unaccountably diverting in his common speech as on the stage.

He particularly excelled as Sir Martin Marall, in the rôle of Gomez in Dryden's *The Spanish Friar* and as Sir Nicholas Cully in Etherege's *Love in a Tub*.

The first part of Dryden's *The Conquest of Granada* was produced at 'The King's House' between 10th December 1670 and the New Year. It was a triumphant success. In the Epilogue the author explains the delay.

> Think him not duller for this years delay;
> He was prepar'd, the women were away;
> And men, without their parts, can hardly play.
> If they, through sickness, seldome did appear,
> Pity the virgins of each theatre!
> For, at both houses, 'twas a sickly year!
> And pity us, your servants, to whose cost;
> In one such sickness, nine whole months are lost.[9]

Both Nell Gwyn of the King's House and Moll Davis had been, of necessity, absent from the theatre, because they were *enceinte*.

How we miss Pepys' description of this play! Evelyn, however, on 9th February 1671, was present at the great ball at Whitehall when Queen Catherine of Braganza and distinguished ladies danced. "Next day was acted there," he wrote, "the famous play call'd 'The Siege of Granada' [*The Conquest of Granada*]. Two days acted successively; there were indeed very glorious scenes and perspectives, the work of Mr. Streeter, who well understands it."[10] Robert Streeter was 'His Majesty's Sergeant Painter'. Dryden dedicated his play to the Duke of York.

Before coming on to the stage to speak the prologue it is likely that Nell Gwyn had heard rumours about "her Charles the Third's" interest in a certain French mademoiselle, who had attended his sister, the Duchess of Orleans, at Dover. She therefore may have been a little piqued, though in a very merry mood, as she appeared on the stage, in an enormous hat the size of a cart-wheel and wearing an even wider waist-belt. She was greeted by the hilarious laughter of the audience, which included her royal lover, the King. The actors themselves could not conceal their merriment. As we know, Nell was rather low of stature. The French would call her *mignonne* or *piquante*, though they must have considered Nell's prologue very bad taste—and so it was. Mrs. Ellen Gwyn is now speaking under the umbrella of her cart-wheel hat. One can imagine the sudden silence before her entry when even the Restoration fops ceased their banter:

> This jeast was first of t'other houses making,
> And, five times try'd, has never fail'd of taking.
> For 'twere a shame a Poet shou'd be kill'd
> Under the shelter of so broad a shield. . . .

Then one feels the electric atmosphere of the theatre and hears the explosive laughter of the spectators. Even the actors giggled.

> This is that hat whose very sight did win yee
> To laugh and clap as though the Devil were in yee.
> As then, for Nokes, so now, I hope you'l be
> So dull, to laugh, once more for love of me. . . .

How well the dramatist understood his audience, and he was well aware, of course, of their special love for Nelly. It is curious to think of Mrs. Ellen Gwyn again cast in a tragic part—that of Almahide, Queen of Granada—but there is no reason to suppose that she did not succeed in this play. Handsome Ned Kynaston played Mahomet Boabdelin, the last King of Granada; while Charles Hart, with his elegant presence, surpassed himself as Almanzor. Little Major Michael Mohun (he was so proud that he had fought for his King), a superb actor, took the part of Abdelmelech, chief of the Abencerrages. Mr. Littlewood appeared as Ferdinand, king of Spain. The remaining important female parts were played by Mrs. Marshall, possibly Beck; Mrs. Bowtell and Mrs. Jeames.

It is certain that Hart would have spoken the lines of Almanzor with a noble dignity.

> I am as free as Nature first made Man,
> 'Ere the base Laws of Servitude began,
> When wild in woods the noble Savage ran.

The poetry in this play is of a melodious beauty, and once again there are tender passages between Almanzor (Hart) and Almahide (Mrs. Ellen Gwyn).

> *Almahide:* Where should I finde the heart to speake one word?
> Your voice, Sir, is as killing as your sword.
> As you have left the lightning of your eye,
> So would you please to lay your thunder by!
> *Almanzor:* I'me pleas'd and pain'd since first her eyes I saw,
> As I were stung with some Tarantula
> Armes, and the dusty field I less admire,
> And soften strangely in some new desire.
> Honour burns in me, not so fiercely bright
> But pale as fires when master'd by the light.

Nell Gwyn's Almahide does not appear to be a long, sustained part.

Dryden was a dramatist of rare versatility, and *The Conquest of Granada* is, perhaps, the finest of his heroic dramas. It is related that Charles II was highly delighted with Nell's performance in this play, and that he now grew more and more enamoured of her.

What were the last words of Mrs. Ellen Gwyn ever spoken on the stage? It is known that when *An Evening's Love* was revived in 1671 she spoke the epilogue.

> But there's no mercy for a guilty Muse:
> For, like a mistress, she must stand or fall,
> And please you to a height, or not at all.

Perhaps for the last time she played Donna Jacintha to Charles Hart's Wildblood.

Residence in Pall Mall

NELL GWYN'S[1] retirement was definitely a loss to the
stage which she had adorned for six years. It was not
without a pang of regret that Nell gave up acting to
become Charles II's mistress. She was an actress with a touch of
genius, who managed to establish without any difficulty a special
kind of intimacy with her audience. So highly was she thought of
that *Secret Love* was not performed until ten years after her retirement, and *The Indian Emperor*, in which she had been so strongly
criticized by Pepys, not for eleven years. She retained, however,
throughout her short life, an ardent love for the theatre and was
always a constant playgoer. Her favourite Shakespearean play was
probably *The Tempest*, since between September and December
1674 she went four times to see it. She would have excelled as
Ariel. During 1675 she visited the theatre to see *King Lear* and,
on two other occasions, *Macbeth* and *Hamlet*.

The *Dictionary of National Biography*[1] is surely mistaken when
it says that, after an absence of six or seven years, Nell returned to
take the part of Angelica Bianca in Mrs. Behn's *Rover* in 1677.
According to this authority, she played Astrea in *The Constant
Nymph* (an anonymous pastoral) and Thalestris in Samuel
Pordage's *Siege of Babylon* in 1678. She is alleged to have appeared
as Lady Squeamish in Thomas Otway's *Friendship in Fashion* and
Lady Knowell in Mrs. Behn's *Sir Patient Fancy*. It is also extremely
unlikely that Nell would play the part of Queen Elizabeth I in
Bank's *Unhappy Favourite* or *The Earl of Essex*, a rôle wholly
unsuited to her talents as a comedian. It is almost certain, as
Dasent surmised, that Nell has been confused with Anne Quin, a
leading actress at 'The King's House'. Nell liked to invite her
friends as her guests to the theatre and, with characteristic gener-

osity, would take side-boxes at the Duke's Theatre for all of them.

Henceforward, as a favourite bedfellow and companion of Charles II, Nell's career was to follow a different but even more dramatic course. Perhaps at first she had qualms that Charles would quickly tire of her, as he had of Moll Davis, but Nell was never one to worry. Her fearless honesty and candour and her hatred of dissimulation attracted the King from the beginning of their liaison. She called herself a whore, although she was always faithful to the King, and was not particularly upset if others referred to her in such a way.

Nell now could afford a coach drawn by four horses, and she naturally had her own coachman. One day she was a little perplexed when she found him fighting another man. On asking him the reason for the quarrel, her sturdy champion replied with a grimace, " 'E called you a whore, madam." Nell emitted a startling oath. "Go to, you blockhead!" she exclaimed. "Never fight in such a cause. If you want to risk your carcase, do so in defence of the truth." "You may not mind being called a whore," replied her coachman, "but I'll not be called a whore's coachman."[2] On another occasion, on 26th February 1679, Nelly was attending the Duke's Playhouse when somebody entered the pit and called her a whore in a loud voice. It so happened that the Earl of Pembroke's younger brother, Mr. Herbert, was present, and, wishing to vindicate her, he hotly drew his sword. She was much beloved, "and there were many swords drawn, and a great hubbub in the house".[3]

When Nell Gwyn first became Charles II's mistress, her former lover Lord Buckhurst was charged with a diplomatic mission to King Louise XIV of France, "a sleeveless errand", as Dryden called it, to get him out of the way. Buckhurst was certainly sent to France, but King Charles really had no need to get rid of this nobleman to whom he was much attached, for Buckhurst's liaison with Nell had been very brief. Although Nell never married, Buckhurst firstly married Mary, the widow of Charles Berkeley Earl of Falmouth, who had been killed in a naval battle and was a friend of Charles II.* His second wife was Mary, a noted beauty, daughter of James Compton third Earl of Northampton.

* Lady Falmouth was also one of Charles's many mistresses.

His third marriage was to a 'Mrs. Roche', a woman of no social importance.

Sir George Etherege was a dilettante and a talented playwright, but, like Rochester, he was also capable of writing scurrilous verses which are in gross ill taste. It is charitable to doubt whether 'The Lady of Pleasure'[4] is genuinely his work. Etherege makes the Duke of Buckingham say:

> Permit me, Sir, to help you to a whore:
> Kiss her but once, you'll ne'er want Cleaveland more.
> She'll fit you to a Hair, all wit, all fire—
> And Impudent to your own Heart's desire
> And more than this, Sir, you'll save money by her.
> She's Buckhurst's whore at present, but you know—
> When sovereign wants a whore, the subject must forego.

It is likely that Buckingham had encouraged Charles II in his new liaison with Nelly to annoy his cousin Barbara, with whom he had quarrelled. That celebrated termagant Barbara Villiers, Countess of Castlemaine, had now been created Duchess of Cleveland.

It has never been sufficiently emphasized that Nell Gwyn possessed a marked maternal streak in her nature. She was almost twenty years younger than Charles II, yet he must have found her, during the last fifteen years of his life, a real comfort when the political situation worsened and he was beset by manifold dangers. True, he had a loving wife to support him, but Nell Gwyn's protective sense would have helped the King on many occasions. To her two sons she was a devoted, wise and ambitious mother.

Towards the end of 1670, Charles II offered Nell a small house towards the eastern end of Pall Mall. A close study of the rate books of St. Martin-in-the-Fields reveals that the rates during 1670–71 for this house were sixteen shillings a year.[5] Shortly afterwards Nell moved to a much larger house, number 79 Pall Mall, now the premises of the Eagle Star Insurance Company. Its history is very interesting. The first house on this site was erected about 1665.[6] On 1st April this mansion, and the one which adjoined it to the west, were assigned by the Earl of St. Alban's trustees to Sir Thomas Clarges. The Earl of St. Alban's trustees then held the Crown lease. At that period the houses were described as "two faire bricke messuages". In 1667 Sir Thomas Clarges sold the easterly of these two leasehold houses to Sir William Coventry, who was, in Evelyn's opinion, "a wise and witty gentleman". According to Henry Savile, a brother of George Savile later Marquess of Halifax, Coventry paid 1,400 pounds for the house. Pepys, who knew Sir William very well and greatly esteemed him, visited him at his house in Pall Mall during October 1667. Coventry only lived there for about three years, for in February 1670 he sold the lease to Nicholas Leke second Earl of Scarsdale, who later, on 21st July 1671, conveyed the lease to George Knevett in trust for Nell Gwyn.

It is related that Nell was annoyed that she had not at once been granted the freehold of 79 Pall Mall. In 1673, for instance, Sir Joseph Williamson, a Secretary of State, was informed that "Madame Gwinn complains she has no house yet". She wittily asserted that, as she had always conveyed free under the Crown and intended in future to do the same, she would not accept the new house till it was conveyed to her by an Act of Parliament. This story is repeated by Dr. Heberden, a resident in Pall Mall during the late seventeenth century, and may well be authentic. We do know for certain that on 1st December 1676 Charles II granted the freehold of 79 Pall Mall to William Chiffinch, his confidential page of the backstairs, and to Martin Folkes, a trustee of the Earl of St. Alban's estate. They in turn conveyed the freehold to Nell Gwyn's trustees, including her friend Laurence Hyde, a younger son of the late Earl of Clarendon, on 6th April 1677. These five deeds[7] are now lodged in the Pierpont Morgan Library in New York.

The object of these deeds was to make some sort of a settlement on Nell Gwyn's younger son, James Lord Beauclerk, who was born on Christmas Day 1671. The property was firstly settled on Nell for life, then upon Lord Beauclerk and his heirs, and, with the remainder, to her elder son Charles, who had been created Earl of Burford. An amusing story has often been related that Nell on one occasion when she was together with her royal lover, shouted to her elder son, "Come hither, you little bastard, and speak to your father." Charles chided his mistress for such unceremonious language. "Nay, Nelly," he said, "do not give the child such a name." Whereupon Nell answered, in her frank fashion, "Your Majesty, what else can I call him?" She was all the more incensed because her French rival Louise de Kéroualle the Duchess of Portsmouth's son had been created Duke of Richmond at the tender age of 3. Whatever the truth of this story may be, her elder son Charles was created Baron Headington and Earl of Burford, both in the county of Oxford. When Charles Beauclerk was aged 14, in 1684, he became the Duke of St. Albans.

Nell Gwyn's new home, 79 Pall Mall, was a stone-built house, long-windowed, with three storeys containing attics for the servants. It had a very pretty garden, which adjoined the King's garden on the site now covered by Marlborough House. So it was extremely convenient for Charles to visit his mistress in Pall Mall. His Majesty was fond of walking very rapidly in St. James's Park. On one occasion, in March 1671, after presenting the King with some sheets of a book, Evelyn joined him in his walk as far as the King's garden. Evelyn invariably mentions Nell Gwyn in a censorious way. He was now deeply shocked when, in his own words,

I both saw and heard a very familiar discourse between . . . and Mrs. Nellie as they call an imprudent comedian, she looking out of her garden on a terrace at the top of the wall, and he standing on ye greene walk under it. I was heartily sorry at this scene. Thence the King walked to the Dutchess of Cleaveland, another lady of pleasure and curse of our nation.*

The former Barbara Castlemaine was now living in splendour at Berkshire House in St. James's, which was later known as Cleveland House. We are today familiar with Cleveland Row, which commemorates Charles's wanton mistress. By 1671 Barbara had largely lost her hold over the King, though he still occasionally visited her. When Barbara flaunted her love of ostentation by driving out in her coach-and-eight, Nell, to ridicule her, went in a coach drawn by eight oxen.

* 1st March.

Even today St. James's Park retains much of its beauty, but it had more enchantment during the Restoration period. Evelyn provides a lively description of Duck Island, particularly of "two Balearian cranes, one of which having had one of his legs broken and cut off above the knee, had a wooden or boxen leg and thigh with a joint so accurately made, that the creature could walk and use it as well as if it had been natural; it was made by a soldier". The park abounded with wild fowl as it does today. Evelyn relates that "there were withy-pots, or nests, for the wild fowl to lay their eggs in, a little above the surface of the water". There is a story that Charles II had the cages of his favourite birds hung from the trees, though it is not authentic. Colley Cibber mentions that Charles's habit of exercising his dogs and feeding his ducks in St. James's Park made him adored by the people.

John Dennis relates, in his *Original Letters*, an amusing story of how William Wycherley became a lover of the Duchess of Cleveland. Wycherley's first play, *Love in a Wood* or *St. James's Park*, was a striking success. One day, when the dramatist was travelling abroad in his coach down Pall Mall towards St. James's, he happened to encounter the Duchess in hers. Barbara, half thrusting her body "out of the chariot", exclaimed jocularly to Wycherley, with a suggestion of insolence, "You, Wycherley, you are the son of a whore." Wycherley was first astounded, until it dawned on him that the Duchess was referring to a part of a song in his play:

> When parents are slaves
> Their brats cannot be any other,
> Great wits and great braves
> Have always a . . . to their mother.

Wycherley then ordered his coachman to turn back and to overtake Barbara in her chariot. When he drew close enough to make himself heard, Wycherley observed, "Madam, you have been pleased to bestow a title on me which generally belongs to the fortunate. Will your Ladyship be at the play tonight?" "Well," replied Barbara, "what if I am there?" "Why, then," said Wycherley, "I will be there to wait on your Ladyship, tho' I disappoint a very fine woman, who has made me an assignation."

Thus began an intimate friendship, which caused further scandal
at court, though King Charles had long ceased to care.

When Nell Gwyn lived at 79 Pall Mall—and it was her London
home for the remainder of her life—it still had a rural atmosphere.
There were one or two haystacks near St. James's Square, while
the north side of Pall Mall was completely open. A hundred and
fifty elm trees had been planted, which made it a sweet shady walk
for those who cared to saunter. It is well known that the game of
pall-mall was first played in the streets of Pall Mall. It was really
an ancestor of our croquet, and the object of the game was to
drive a wooden ball through an iron ring. Pall Mall in Nell
Gwyn's day was a resort where fashionable ladies in "flame-
coloured taffetas" and fops in periwigs, and wearing scented
gloves, desported themselves.

Nell Gwyn was fond of entertaining her royal lover and her
theatrical friends in her home. Colley Cibber relates a lively story
concerning one of these parties of pleasure.[8] Nell adored music,
and nothing endeared her more to Charles II than the concerts,
which she organized. At one of them she obtained the services of a
young man, Henry Bowman,* who was renowned for his exquisite voice. There was a small but distinguished audience,
including James Duke of York, nicknamed among Nell's circle of
friends as 'dismal Jimmy'. When the concert was over, Charles II
expressed himself in his usual gracious way as highly delighted
with the performance. "Then, Sir," said Nell Gwyn, in her impulsive way, which made her so attractive to the male sex, "to show
you don't speak like a courtier, I hope you will make the performers a handsome present." The King, momentarily non-
plussed, had to admit, which was almost always the case, that he
had no money about him, and, turning to the Duke of York, he
asked, "And you, brother?" The Duke answered, "I believe, Sir,
not above a guinea or two." Nell then convulsed her friends by
assuming her most comical expression and making bold with the
King's favourite phrase. "Odsfish!" she cried, "what company
am I got into!" No doubt a suitable reminder to the King of
Nelly's supper with him, the Duke of York and Villiers in a tavern
after the theatre some years before. Nell's intimate supper parties

* 1651-1739.

to the King, and to members of "the merry gang", were extremely gay, and politicians eagerly sought invitations to them. On one occasion she wanted to give a party for the King's birthday, 29th May. Since Nell was on friendly terms with the ravishing Maria Brudenell Countess of Shrewsbury, mistress of the Duke of Buckingham, it was hinted to her by the King that she might include Lady Shrewsbury among the guests. Nell retorted in her characteristic way: "One whore at a time is enough for you, Sire."

Lady Shrewsbury's parties were very gay. Lord Conway wrote to Arthur Capel, Earl of Essex at the end of November 1673 that My Lord Treasurer (Lord Clifford of Chudleigh) had carried him by chair to My Lady Shrewsbury's house in King Street, Westminster where he encountered Nell Gwyn, the Duke of Buckingham and Mr. Speaker Seymour. They supped at 3 a.m. "and drank smartly".

The Army and Navy Club in Pall Mall possesses some fascinating relics of Nell Gwyn, including some interesting portraits. There is a silver fruit knife (1680),* and it is tempting to imagine Nelly using it at one of her gay supper parties to skin a peach or eat a fig. There is displayed her miniature in a case, which once belonged to Charles II. It is placed under the different little mica slips depicting her in her various characters and costumes.

The club also possesses a collection of Nell's household bills,[10] which throw little gleams of light on her activities as a hostess and on her character. Sir Charles Petrie, in a fascinating article published by the *Illustrated London News*,† refers to these housekeeping accounts. For instance, there is a bill from Nell's poulterer for March 1676. Six ducklings cost £1 10s, while four geese cost £2; '6 Rabets' cost 7s and two chickens 4s, two leaverets 4s, one duckling 5s and 6 fat chickens 12s. How one envies Nell's guests. Another curious account in 1675 is 'for a pidgeon pey' 2s 6d, and a bottle of canary 2s 6d. Contrary to what one might expect, Nell was usually prompt in paying her household accounts, no doubt mindful that her poulterer and her upholsterer could seldom afford to wait long for payment. A receipt signed by Thomas Parry shows that she paid this account two months and

* Presented by Captain Philp, late of the Scots Greys, in 1888.
† 14th January 1956.

three days after it was incurred. There is an account from a chairman of a sedan-chair: 'For careing you yesterday, and wayting eleven oures, 11s 6d.' This seems a very moderate fee for such a long wait, but the chairman may have considered it an honour to wait for Mrs. Nelly. She bought half a pound of tea at 28s per pound, which is excessive. A teapot cost 16s. Another account, presented in 1675, is 'for three pieces of silk, one for yourself, another for your sister, and another for your woman'. This was Nell's sister Rose, now Mrs. Cassells. A bill for £1 17s, incurred for fruit, included figs and a basket of grapes. Nell was very partial to figs. Another curious item is a receipt for a bill paid in 1675 for 'two childrens caps'—presumably for her two sons.

One ton of coal cost £1 12s. There is a receipted account from an upholsterer, Anne Traherne, for £74 4s 3d, including 'the exchange of a glase for yr Dressing Rome £7. For gilding the hinges and Nayles for a cabinett £3 10s.' For Carriage decorations 'The Honble. Madame Gwinne' had to pay £146 5s. For a drapery bill incurred in September 1675, 'Madam Gwinne' had to pay Peter Prettye £3 8s 11d. Among the documents are a receipted 'coachman's bill' for fodder and wages amounting to £22 18s.

Perhaps the most human document in this collection is an advertisement in the *London Gazette* of 16th–19th July 1673. It reads:

A small liver coloured Spanish Bitch lost from the King's lodgings, on the 14th instant, with a little white on her breast and a little white on the tops of her hind feet. Whoever brings her to Mr. Chiffinch's lodgings at the King's Back-Stairs, or to the King's Dog-Keeper in St. James's Park shall be well rewarded for their pains.

It is especially tantalizing since we never know whether or not the King's pet was recovered.

Nell was always devoted to her old mother, Madame Gwyn, even if she continued to souse herself with brandy. For some time she seems to have lived with her daughter in Pall Mall, for there exists an apothecary's bill for "plasters, glysters, and cordials" sent to Pall Mall for the purpose of restoring the old lady to health. Nell also maintained close relations with her sister Rose, now Mrs. Cassells, for her name is included in an account sent to Nell Gwyn by the chairman of a public sedan-chair. We know that she bought her own sedan-chair in January 1675, that it was an elaborate one with fine gold carvings and that it cost her £34 11s. All the same, Nell sometimes used a public chair, and no doubt her chairman never minded waiting for such a charming and witty person, provided his accounts were promptly paid. Nell Gwyn was a kind and considerate friend to those whom she cherished, and she occasionally loaned her chair to her friend Lady Sandys when she wanted to visit the theatre at Whitehall. Nell's friends at Court included most of the gay sparks, such as Harry Killigrew ('Lying Killigrew' as he was called), who had once befriended her sister Rose when in trouble; the Duke of Bucks; John Sheffield Earl of Mulgrave, who dabbled in poetry; John Wilmot Earl of Rochester; and his great friend, Henry Savile. Her favourite politician was Laurence Hyde, and the acquaintance was to ripen into a cherished friendship.

Nell felt extremely sad when she heard of the disastrous fire, which occurred on 25th January 1671, destroying part of 'The King's House', or Theatre Royal, where she had so often delighted the people with her wit and acting. The fire almost certainly began under the stairs, where Orange Moll stored her fruit. By 26th March 1674 a new theatre had been built to replace the original 'King's House'.

When Nell's second son was born, on Christmas Day in 1671, he was christened James, as a mark of respect to James Duke of York. The King's younger brother had not yet publicly ack-nowledged himself to be a Catholic, but he was known to be a secret one. Despite Nell's robust Protestantism, the Duke seems to have liked her and never resented her influence with his brother, the King, as he later feared the Duchess of Portsmouth's.

When Nell's elder son, the Earl of Burford, was about 10, Thomas Otway, the celebrated dramatist, was appointed his tutor. He was born in Sussex in 1652 and educated at Winchester College and Christ Church, Oxford. The tragedy of Otway's life was his unrequited passion for the beautiful actress, Mrs. Elizabeth Barry, who treated his advances with disdain. She became the mistress of John Wilmot second Earl of Rochester, who indeed trained her for the stage. Otway's supreme effort in tragedy is, perhaps, *Venice Preserved*★ (1682), which was acted at the Duke's Theatre and often revived. He was ruined by his craving for drink and by his obsession for Mrs. Barry, to whom he sent piteous love letters. When Nell appointed Otway tutor to her elder son, he had just completed *The Souldier's Fortune*. On 1st June 1680, the dramatist witnessed a power of attorney enabling Mrs. Ellen Gwyn to receive her pension. At the age of 12, Lord Burford was sent by his father and mother to Paris, where Richard Graham Viscount Preston, a staunch Tory who had succeeded Henry Savile as ambassador in 1682, supervised his French studies.

Nell, after she became Charles II's mistress, would never brook any nonsense from the rakes who abounded at court. Colbert de Croissy, the French ambassador in London, informed† his Foreign Minister, M. Pomponne, that the Duke of Buckingham, having one morning entered the King's apartments to discuss state affairs with his Majesty, found Nell there. The Duke endeavoured to persuade her to grant him her favours without success, for when he rumpled the collar of her dress while trying to kiss her, she soundly boxed his ears. All the same she was attached to the 'Duke of Bucks', as he was often called. Girolamo Alberti, Venetian Secretary in England, reported to the Doge and Senate: "Buckingham is now in disgrace with the King for an audacious attempt on His Majesty's private pleasures."[11] This clearly reveals that Charles was capable of jealousy where Nell was concerned.

When Lord Cavendish, who later became first Duke of Devonshire, tried to make love to Nelly, the King was annoyed and forbade her to have anything to do with him. It is probable, however, that her rival, Louise de Kéroualle Duchess of Portsmouth, was unfaithful to Charles II on two occasions, though the position is a little obscure.

The relations between Nell and Louise at the Court of Charles II are of fascinating interest, and the letters to the French Foreign Ministers from Colbert de Croissy and one of his successors as French Ambassador in London, Honoré de Courtin, concerning this subject, are entertaining and lively.

★ Otway dedicated it to the Duchess of Portsmouth.
† 23rd January 1672.

The Rival Mistresses

URING the night of 29th June 1670, Charles II's beloved Minette, Madame of France, died in agony at Saint-Cloud only three weeks after she had returned to France from Dover. When Charles heard the news from Sir Thomas Armstrong, an emissary from Ralph Montagu, the English Ambassador in Paris, his dark saturnine face betrayed overwhelming grief. He said, with unusual vehemence, "Monsieur* is a villain! But, Sir Thomas, I beg of you not to say a word of this to others." John Wilmot Earl of Rochester wrote to his wife in Oxfordshire: "The King endures the highest affliction imaginable."[1] At first it was thought that Madame had been poisoned, but today it is almost certain that she was a victim of cholera morbus.

Colbert de Croisy feared lest the hopes based on the Treaty of Dover between the two countries would be altogether blighted. A distinguished soldier, the Maréchal de Bellefonds, was charged by Louis XIV to convey his official condolences to Charles, while the mercurial Duke of Buckingham during July was sent on a delicate mission to Versailles. The purpose of his journey was partly political, but he had been instructed by Charles II to renew the offer made to Louise de Kéroualle at Dover, that she should come to England, where she would be appointed a maid-of-honour to Queen Catherine of Braganza. Mlle de Kéroualle, at 21, was dark, very pretty, with a soft voice. She was very conscious of her noble birth. Even as a young girl she was shrewd and calculating, and possessed an *esprit froid*. When Buckingham told her of his master's offer, Louise assured him that her grief was so great at the death of Madame that her only desire was to enter a convent. When Louis XIV—her sovereign—entreated her to

* Philippe Duc d'Orléans, the effeminate younger brother of Louis XIV.

accept the King of England's offer, Louise eventually agreed to accompany the Duke of Buckingham on his homeward journey. That nobleman, with characteristic lack of consideration, or owing to absence of mind, is said to have left Mlle de Kéroualle stranded at Dieppe for two weeks.

Charles II, however, eager to see once again the young French girl, who had so attracted him in Dover, sent one of his royal yachts to transport her to England. It was now autumn, and Louise was appointed a maid-of-honour to Catherine of Braganza, much to the Queen's chagrin. Charles welcomed Mlle de Kéroualle all the more because she was a link with his beloved Minette. There were sentimental memories of his sister at Versailles and Saint-Cloud, and Louise, with her soft, musical voice was not loath to talk of her former mistress to please the King. When she had gained more experience, Louise acquired a French woman's dexterity in studying the King's tastes so that she might maintain her hold over him and please him in all ways. Charles was extremely attentive to her, provided for her luxurious apartments in Whitehall Palace, and it was obvious to the expectant courtiers that he wanted to make her his mistress. Nell Gwyn, and his old flame Barbara Duchess of Cleveland, prepared to resist the French intruder.

Meanwhile Louise played her cards with consummate finesse. She willingly listened to the King's ardent declarations of affection, while carefully refraining from committing herself in any way. The French Ambassador, Colbert de Croissy, was closely watching the situation, and reported to his Minister of War, Louvois:*

> The influence of the Duchess (Cleveland) visibly wanes . . . While she loses favour, the King of England's fancy for Mademoiselle de Kéroualle grows stronger. The attacks of nausea she had yesterday, when dining with me, makes me hope I shall find in her a useful ally as long as my embassy lasts.†

Colbert de Croissy was deluding himself with false hopes, since Louise's nausea was owing to a slight fever and not to the cause suspected. The young girl, with her baby face, and air of innocence, was still a virgin.

* François-Michel Le Tellier, Marquis de Louvois.
† Colbert de Croissy to Louvois, 21st September 1671.

To overcome the supposed scruples of Mademoiselle de Kéroualle one of the King's ministers, Henry Bennet Lord Arlington, and his Dutch-born wife resorted to a plot. The King was in the habit of attending the horse-matches at Newmarket each autumn, and that favourite haunt of Charles II lay within a convenient distance of the Arlington's resplendent country seat, Euston. What could be more natural than to invite Louise de Kéroualle and the French Ambassador together with their other guests? The King would certainly visit Euston during his sojourn at Newmarket, where he could enjoy the society of his new favourite, although Louise, unlike Nelly, never cared for sport. Charles continued to load her with presents, and the courtiers wagered how long Mademoiselle de Kéroualle would be able to continue her resistance.

It so happened that John Evelyn was among Lord Arlington's guests during October 1671, and what he writes in his diary strongly suggests that Louise became the King's mistress on this occasion.[2] In his puritanical way Evelyn deeply deplored what had occurred.

It was universally reported that the Faire Lady—was bedded one of these nights, and the stocking flung, after the manner of a married bride; I acknowledge she was for the most part in her undresse all day, and that there was a fondnesse and toying with that young wanton; nay, 'twas said I was at the former ceremony, but 'tis utterly false. . . . However, 'twas with confidence believed she was made a *Misse*, as they call these unhappy creatures, with solemnity at this time.

Forneron, in his biography of Louise de Kéroualle, quotes the young Frenchwoman's exact words: "Me no bad woman. If me taut me was one bad woman, me would cut mine own trote." They sound convincing enough, considering the short time she had been in England. It is obvious that some sort of mock wedding was staged at Euston. One can imagine the sly glances exchanged between the courtiers and the dawning arrogance of Mlle de Kéroualle, now that she shared the King's bed. Her modesty vanished like the thawing of snow. Colbert de Croissy was too sanguine in his belief that the King's passion for her would exclude all other attachments, but he was correct in thinking that it would prove a long one.

On 30th March 1672, Madame de Sévigné, who was always extremely well-informed about the English court, referred to Mlle de Kéroualle in a letter to her daughter, the Countess de Grignan:

Querouaille, whose fortune had been predicted before she left this kingdom, has fully verified it: The K . . . of England was passionately fond of her, and she, on her side, had no aversion to him: In short, she is now about eight months gone with child. Poor Castlemaine is turned off: Such is the fate of mistresses in that Kingdom.

She might have added, remembering the obscurity of Louise de la Vallière when Louis XIV tired of her, "such is also the fate of mistresses in our Court". Nobody was surprised when Louise de Kéroualle gave birth to an infant son, exactly nine months after her visit to Euston, on 29th July 1672. He was named Charles Lennox and was later recognized and created Duke of Richmond. The title was now vacant, since Charles Stuart sixth Duke of Lennox and third Duke of Richmond, husband of La Belle Stuart, had recently died in December 1672 at Elsinore in Denmark.

It must be admitted that Nell Gwyn owed some of her popularity among the English people to the fact that her French rival was detested as a sly intriguer in the interests of France, a spy and an avaricious hoarder of the King's money. Since they could not pronounce her name, they nicknamed her 'Madame Carwell'. Yet Louise on the whole was a less disagreeable character than her predecessor, Barbara Countess of Castlemaine. She possessed artistic taste though no particular taste in literature.

Nell naturally detested her in a robust British way, and never lost any opportunity of mocking Louise or making her seem foolish in the eyes of the King. She nicknamed Louise 'Sqintabella', because she had a slight cast in one of her eyes, or would refer to her rival as 'The Weeping Willow', since she usually resorted to the female expedient of tears when she wanted something from 'Chanticleer', as Charles II was sometimes called at court. It has been questioned whether Nelly would have dared to have used these nicknames in 'Chanticleer's' presence, but it is very likely that she did later on, especially when the King's passion for the lady had waned a little. For his part, Charles's nickname for his French favourite was 'Fubbs' after she had put on some weight. A ship of the Royal Navy was named after her, the *Fubbs Yacht*, and there was a public house at Greenwich of the same name. A resplendent bed was especially brought over in the Cleveland yacht for the use of Louise and, no doubt, her royal paramour.

Nell and Louise were destined to be rivals, for they were complete contrasts. Their enmity certainly made Charles II's court more lively. Nell Gwyn was clever, warm-hearted, indiscreet, generous, vulgar and confided too freely in worthless people; while Louise was an insufferable snob, intelligent, not intellectual, cold, calculating and sufficiently diplomatic to be able to keep a secret. As a Roman Catholic she was also an object of hostility to the English people.

Manuscripts[3] in the Dean's Cloister, Windsor Castle, reveal that Mrs. Elinor Gwyn of the parish of St. Martin-in-the-Fields was appointed, during 1675, one of the ladies of Her Majesty the Queen's Privy Chamber. Nell Gwyn never occupied rooms in the Palace of Whitehall, for her own house in Pall Mall was conveniently situated near Whitehall. There is no reason to suppose that Nell ever conducted herself in a disrespectful manner towards Catherine of Braganza, who, during the 1670s, was living mostly in Somerset House in the Strand. Sir John Reresby relates in his memoirs, however, that Louise de Kéroualle after she had been created Duchess of Portsmouth,* upset Catherine of Braganza on one occasion in Windsor Castle when she entered her apartments as a lady of the bedchamber to wait on her, which she had the good taste very seldom to do. Tears welled in the eyes of the poor wronged queen, while Louise laughed gently but in her maddening way.

There is little doubt that Louise hated Nell Gwyn and sometimes nagged her royal lover for having the ill taste to make a former orange-wench his mistress. It seemed incredible to Louise,

---

* Louise de Kéroualle was created Baroness of Petersfield, Countess of Farnham and Duchess of Portsmouth in 1673.

as a foreigner, that Charles showed no inclination to get rid of the vulgar, common creature. After all, she herself had noble Breton blood in her veins. Why did the King demean himself by taking to his bed this upstart actress? The snobbery of her French rival infuriated Nelly. Her deadly barbs were designed to ridicule Louise in the eyes of Charles II and the whole court.

For instance, when Louise heard of the execution during 1682 of the Chevalier de Rohan, who came of a distinguished French family, she assumed deep mourning, although in fact she was no relation of the Chevalier's. Next day the courtiers were greatly surprised when Nell Gwyn also appeared dressed in deepest black. One of the courtiers, curious to discover the reason for her funeral dress, asked her for whom she wore this unaccustomed mourning. "Why!" answered Nell in her cheeky fashion, "have you not heard of my loss in the death of the Cham of Tartary?" She explained, "I was exactly the same relation to the Cham of Tartary, as the Duchess of Portsmouth was to the Chevalier de Rohan." Louise was present and heard the whole conversation. When the incident was reported to Charles II he was richly amused.

When the King of Sweden died, Louise at once went into mourning, although she was not related. Shortly afterwards the King of Portugal conveniently died, and Nell dressed in black and ordered that her coach should be bedecked in mourning. Louise complained to King Charles, who, in order to make peace between his two mistresses, made the sensible suggestion that Louise should have all the kings of the north, while Nell retained all the kings of the south. Another version of this story says that Nell herself met her rival one day in her coach, and proposed to her: "Let us agree to divide the world, you shall have the kings of the north, and I the kings of the south."

Nobody has written a more amusing description of the rivalry between the two favourites than the Marchioness de Sévigné. She wrote to her daughter on 11th September 1675:

With regard to England, Mademoiselle de Kéroualle has not been disappointed in anything she proposed; she desired to be a mistress to the King, and she is so. He lodges with her almost every night in the face of all the whole Court: She has had a son, who has been acknowledged, and presented with two dutchies. She amasses treasure, and makes herself feared and respected by as many as she can. But she did not foresee that she should find a young actress [Nell Gwyn] in her way, whom the King doats on; and she had it not in her power to withdraw him from her. He divides his care, his time, and his health between these two. The actress is as haughty as Mademoiselle; she insults her, she makes grimaces at her, she attacks her, she frequently steals the King from her, and boasts whenever he gives her the preference. She is young, indiscreet, confident, wild, and of an agreeable humour; she sings, she dances, she acts her part with a good grace. She has a son by the King, and hopes to have him acknowledged. As to Mademoiselle, she reasons thus: this dutches says she, pretends to be a person of quality. If she be a lady of such quality, why does she demean herself to be a courtesan? She ought to die for shame. As for me, it is my profession; I do not pretend to anything better. The King entertains me, and I am constant to him at present. He has a son by me; I pretend that he ought to acknowledge him, and I am well assured he will, for he loves me as well as he does Mademoiselle. This creature gets the upper hand, and discountenances, and embarrasses the dutchess extremely. I like these original characters. . . .

Madame de Sévigné described the exact position with lucidity and wit. Charles II loved both Nell Gwyn and the Duchess of Portsmouth in his own peculiar way.

A study of the Secret Service payments of Charles II during 1679 and later, and of his successor James II from 30th March to 25th December 1688, reveals that the Duchess of Portsmouth received a great deal of money from the King. Typical items are: "To the Dutchess of Portsmouth, for a quarter ended at Michael' 1679, £3,000. To Dr. Taylor, for the use of the Dutchess of Portsmouth, £1,250."[5] In comparison the amounts paid to Mrs. Ellen Gwyn are small.

Nell was generous and kind-hearted by temperament, and, unlike Barbara Villiers and Louise de Kéroualle, certainly far from avaricious. On one occasion when she was abroad in her coach, Nell noticed a clergyman being taken to prison. She inquired the reason. Having been told that it was for debt, she herself paid the sum owed, thus gaining for the wretched man his freedom. As already stated, during the first four years of her liaison with Charles II, she received 60,000 pounds from her royal lover. This is indeed a large amount of money, but far more was squandered on the French favourite. Andrew Marvell, the satirical poet, who wrote bitter poems about Charles II, relates that the King granted to Louise the wine licenses, which brought her 10,000 pounds a year. In one year Louise received the fantastic amount of 136,668 pounds. Marvel makes the King say, in one of his satires, *Royal Resolution*:

> I'll wholly abandon all public affairs,
> And pass all my time with buffoons and players,
> And saunter to Nelly when I should be at prayers.

The *Calendar of Treasury Books* reveals that Nell received regular payments of 1,000 pounds on Lady Day 30th March 1675, and of 500 pounds on other occasions. On 18th February appears the interesting item: Charles Bertie to pay Mrs. Gwinn 500 pounds, "which is not to be accounted any part of her allowance". Between 31st December 1674 and 30th April 1675, Charles gave her 2,500 pounds from the Secret Service Funds as "Bounty".

Small wonder that Charles II sometimes complained of his financial difficulties. We find Nell during 1675 offering a witty suggestion how the King might well solve his troubles. When Parliament reassembled, she told him, "Why not present them with a 'Scotch Collop', a 'French ragoût', and a 'calf's head'? That would surely be the best means of extracting money from them." The 'Scotch Collop' was the red-haired Duke of Lauderdale,* a former member of the Cabal ministry, whom Nell detested. Lauderdale was given sumptuous apartments in Whitehall on the northern side of the stone gallery, south of the privy gardens. For some years his political influence in Whitehall was immense, particularly with regard to Scottish affairs. The 'French ragoût' was, of course, her rival the Duchess of Portsmouth; and the 'Calf's Head' was, perhaps, Robert Spencer Earl of Sunderland. It is, however, difficult to understand why Sunderland was referred to as the 'Calf's head', for he was a handsome man, with fair hair, dark, slanting eyes and an effeminate mouth.

Was Nell Gwyn extravagant? She certainly had luxurious tastes.

---

* 1616-1682. Created Duke of Lauderdale by Charles II in 1672.

Peter Cunningham relates that she possessed a magnificent silver bedstead which she bought from her silversmith John Coques in 1764. The total amount of this bill, which has been preserved, came to £1,135 3s 1d. Nell's bedstead was elaborately decorated with ornaments of silver, such as the King's head, slaves, crowns, Cupid and Jacob Hall dancing upon a rope of wire-work. Nell often invited her friends to the theatre, and she would hire sedan-chairs to take them. Her dainty white satin petticoats and white and red satin nightgowns were objects of envy to her women friends, and a French ambassador on one occasion expressed delight and astonishment at their variety. Nell had a feminine fondness for beautiful things; for exquisite fans and pairs of satin shoes laced over with gold. With the King as her lover, it was natural that she should want to satisfy her desire to possess cherished possessions, which had been denied her when she played, half-starved, in the London streets.

Nell Gwyn was a guest of Charles II when he gave a *souper dansant* for the Count of Neuberg,* who was visiting England during the summer of 1675. He was the son and heir of the Count Palatine of Neuberg, who had entertained Charles most hospitably during his exile, when he visited Dusseldorf. The King had esteemed this German princeling and was now anxious to return the hospitality to the Count of Neuberg. Nell was in high spirits at a reception in the prince's honour, which was held in the Queen's private apartments. His suite numbered fifty persons, though he desired to remain incognito.[6] It happened to be an excessively hot summer night, and the courtiers under their heavy periwigs were perspiring freely. The King, a considerate host, though possibly it was Nell's idea, suggested to his guests that they should all sally forth from the palace into St. James's Park, where they could dance by the light of the moon. With the soft breezes stirring the trees, the teasing of the violins and the lovely satin dresses of the ladies, it was an enchanted scene. A night for elves and fairies to be abroad, and Nell was in a mischievous mood.

After the dancing was over, the King suggested to the Prince of Neuberg and the lords and ladies of his household that they should go in his royal barge up the river to Hampton Court. It

* Philip William.

was already dawn, and nobody thought of bed. Charles was a keen
fisherman and now brought out his rod to try his luck. The King
had no success and was just about to abandon his efforts when
Nell with a sprightly laugh urged him: "But see, Sire, you have
got a bite at last." Sure enough, when the King pulled in his rod,
he found half a dozen fried smelts at the end of the line, tied to
his hook with a silken thread. Nell declared, amid much laughter,
that while humble fishermen must catch their fish alive, such a
great king must have his fish ready for eating. The Prince of
Neuberg was certainly agreeably surprised when, on pulling in
his line—and he did so with great difficulty—he found not only a
purse of gold, containing precious stones, but also a miniature of a
lady with whom he was much enamoured. Such pranks as these
endeared Nell all the more to Charles II, for he could never
resist her jests.

Nell's rival, the Duchess of Portsmouth, had splendid apartments in the Palace at Whitehall. Evelyn, who visited them by
chance during September 1675,* considered that they were
"luxuriously furnished, and with ten times the richnesse and glory
beyond the Queene's". There we can imagine her, admiring
herself in her mirror, with her babylike face, black eyes, and her
hair puffed in small ringlets about her face. If only she could
continue to give Louis XIV valuable services, he might grant her
the coveted distinction of a stool, or tabouret, of duchess in the
presence-chamber at the French court at Versailles. This was the
consummate ambition of the scheming Bretonne. In her sumptuous apartments she incessantly intrigued with Lord Danby† and
other politicians in the interests of France, and her own interests.
It is possible that Louise later granted Danby a share of her
favours.

On one occasion Louise ordered a silversmith, who possessed a
shop on the north side of Pall Mall, to provide her with a splendid
service of silver. It seems likely that the silversmith in question
was John Coques, who had made the silver bedstead for Nell
Gwyn. The French favourite was so hated by the people of
London, that they collected outside the silversmith's shop, loudly

---

* 10th September.
† Sir Thomas Osborne, created Earl of Danby, later Duke of Leeds.

complaining that the service of silver should have been given 'Mrs. Nelly' rather than 'Madame Carwell'.

Hester Chapman, in her interesting work *Privileged Persons*, states that the French favourite was "even more disliked than Nell Gwynne, whose consciously exploited cockney insolence was much resented by the class from which she sprang". This is surely too sweeping an opinion, for contemporary accounts clearly reveal that Nell's popularity with the people was enhanced owing to their hatred for the Duchess of Portsmouth. The rare criticism of 'Mrs. Nelly' usually came from men in positions of authority.

During 1676 Henri de Massue, Marquis de Ruvigny, was succeeded as French Ambassador in London by a subtle diplomat named Honoré de Courtin, Seigneur de Chanteroine, who had been Councillor of the Parliament of Rouen at the age of 14. He was now aged 49, a little dapper man from Normandy, very gallant in his attentions to the ladies and well equipped to play his part unravelling the intrigues which encompassed the court of Charles II. He was extremely resourceful, tactful and possessed a ripe judgment. His witty letters, full of humour, to various French Foreign Ministers about Charles II's mistresses are a source of delight to those who read them.

Towards the end of 1675 there arrived in England a notorious Roman lady of a rare beauty. This was Hortense Mancini Duchess of Mazarin, youngest and favourite niece of the late Cardinal Mazarin. This eccentric and brilliant woman, who had led a strange wandering life in Europe, had come to London, it was said, with the express intention of becoming Charles II's mistress. When she reached London she was dressed in male costume and attended by a train of seven servants. Her sojourn there was to cause Louise de Kéroualle more anxiety and annoyance than even the frank taunts of Nell Gwyn had done.

Triumph of a Roman Lady

WHEN the Duchess Mazarin arrived in London, the comedian 'Mistris Nesle' (as Courtin delightfully refers to her) at once wore mourning to mark the eclipse of Her Grace of Portsmouth, but Nell was mistaken, as events will shortly show. The intrigues of Ralph Montagu,* who had known Hortense intimately in Chambery, were mainly responsible for her coming to London. Montagu was an implacable enemy of the Duchess of Portsmouth and wished to encompass her downfall, so that Hortense might supplant her in the King's affections. Hortense had left her husband, Armand de la Porte Le Duc Mazarin, though she was acutely worried by her financial affairs. Hortense was one of the most lovely and intelligent women of her age, her hair jet-black and curled, while her complexion was dark and Italianate. Her eyes were, perhaps, her loveliest feature, neither blue nor grey, nor altogether black, but a mixture of all three.[1] Some men, however, would prefer the hazel eyes of Nell Gwyn.

It so happened that Hortense was related, through her Martinozzi cousins, to the young Duchess of York, who as Maria D'Este di Modena had married her husband in 1673. She first stayed as the guest of the Duke and Duchess in St. James's Palace, until the Duke placed at her disposal a house in St. James's Park, which he now owned. It was easy for Charles II to visit his sister-in-law, who was *enceinte*, and there he would often see the lovely Hortense, now aged 29. Old memories were kindled and revived, for Charles, as an exiled king in Europe, had once wanted to marry her.

* As English Ambassador in France in 1670 he was present when Henrietta Duchess of Orleans died.

Hortense's arrival caused a tremendous sensation at court. Many of the courtiers fell in love with her, while the ladies at first regarded her with jealousy, until they too succumbed to her charm. When the French Ambassador encountered the distinguished Portuguese statesman, the Conde de Castelmelhor,* during a nocturnal walk in St. James's Park in early July 1676 about eleven, he felt sorry for him, "because he is dying for love of Madame Mazarin". There was a strong faction at Court who detested Louise de Kéroualle, and they thought of Hortense as their natural ally against the French favourite.

Disconsolate, and fearing that her own position was in peril—as indeed it was—the Duchess of Portsmouth, in poor health, departed for Bath on 25th May (1676) to drink the waters, where she stayed for six weeks. On her return to London, Nell Gwyn jested that she would have to arm herself to the teeth against Louise's resentment, owing to the frequent visits Charles had paid her during Louise's absence in Bath.[2] Three days after her return Louise gave a diplomatic musical party. The musicians of Louis XIV's chamber, including Lambert, the father-in-law of Lulli, and three musicians named La Forest, Gandomeche, and Gilet, who were visiting England, performed at her request. When Charles II entered her apartments, Louise made a fool of herself by asking the musicians to sing a Spanish song: '*Mate me con no mirar, mas ne me mate con zelos.*'† Edmund Waller wrote a poem called 'The Triple Combat', which describes in a lively way the rivalry between the three ladies, Little Britain (Portsmouth), The Amazon (Mazarin), and Chloris (Nell Gwyn).

> The lovely Chloris well attended came,
> A thousand Graces waited on the dame:
> Her matchless form made all the English glad,
> And foreign beauties less assurance had. . . .

Meanwhile Honoré de Courtin, the French Ambassador, needed all his diplomatic finesse to soothe the hurt feelings of the Duchess

---

* Don Luis de Vasconcellos, an intimate friend of Queen Catherine of Braganza. He had quarrelled with Pedro II and had taken refuge in England.
† "Kill me by not looking at me, but do not kill me with jealousy."

of Portsmouth. On one occasion when he visited her in her apartments in Whitehall, he found her weeping, attended by two French maids. "Madame La Duchesse," he implored her, "I do beg you to conceal your chagrin, and seem not to mind the King's altered humour." Courtin, however, was wily enough to make friends with the Duchesse Mazarin, and it is evident from his letters to his Foreign Minister that this middle-aged diplomat was not insensible to her charms. He was instructed by Louis XIV to ascertain what the Duchesse Mazarin's real intentions were towards the French king. Louvois, not without a touch of malice, referred to the stories from London that Courtin had lost his heart to Hortense.

The summer of 1676 was warm and agreeable, engendering light thoughts of dalliance and love, even among the elderly. Courtin told Louvois that it was essential to be an *homme de plaisir* in England, or not to come there at all. To him it seemed evident that Hortense was now Charles II's mistress. They were constantly together, and the King gave gay parties on the river in her honour. Only when he went up the river to bathe every evening did he go without her. Courtin reported to Louis XIV: "The ladies do not go with the men . . . it is the only decency which they observe in this country. There is a great deal of laxness in the rest of their conduct."[3] The French king was amused by his ambassador's account of the Duchess of Portsmouth's tears, and now called her 'La Signora Adolorada'. Courtin, observing narrowly the habits of the English king, noticed that he did not return to his apartments until three o'clock in the morning. Courtin guessed that the King was mostly with Madame de Mazarin. If only William Chiffinch had written a journal, we should know for certain where Charles passed those delectable hours. Even Nelly probably felt neglected during these summer months. Yet she would have rejoiced that 'the weeping willow'—as she referred to the Duchess of Portsmouth—was apparently no longer in favour.

Nelly, however, had nothing to complain of. During the autumn the King often passed the nights with her and visited her more often than the Duchess of Portsmouth. The well-informed Courtin told his Foreign Minister:

I have ascertained beyond doubt that he passes nights much less often with her (the Duchess of Portsmouth) than with Mistris Nesle; and, if I can believe those who are most about with him, his relations with the Duchess of Portsmouth have subsided into a virtuous friendship. As to the Duchess Mazarin, I know he thinks her the finest woman that he ever saw in his life. . . .

In a few of his letters, Courtin again quaintly refers to Nell Gwyn as 'Mistris Nesle'. It is evident that she intrigued him. He was aware, however, that Mistris Nesle's influence in political matters was negligible and that the conversation at the agreeable supper parties of "the frisking comedian" was confined to frivolities and free from restraint.

The ambassador's own special favourite was Jane Middleton, who he considered the most beautiful woman in England. He wrote to the Marquis de Louvois, one of his best friends: "I would give her all your money if she would only listen to my suit, but she once refused a purse of fifteen hundred pounds offered her by Monsieur de Gramont, so you need not fear for your treasure."[4] Jane Middleton, with her lovely auburn hair and exquisite figure, was the daughter of Sir Robert Needham. She became a skilful amateur artist and married Charles Middleton of Ruabon in 1660.

Hortense had a fascinating personality; it was not only men who succumbed to her charm. The young Anne Fitzroy, Countess of Sussex, the elder of the natural daughters of Charles II by Barbara Villiers,* formed a great friendship with her, and the two became almost inseparable. Lady Sussex was hardly more than a child, although already married. She delighted in games of battledore and shuttlecock with Hortense in the French Ambassador's withdrawing-room. He occupied a house, Number 8 York Street, off St. James's Square. Courtin was well aware that Charles II found his daughter's rooms in Whitehall convenient for his secret assignations with the Duchesse de Mazarin. They lay immediately above the King's apartments and were the same rooms which had been formerly occupied by the Duchess of Cleveland. Nobody possessed the master-key except Charles and William Chiffinch.

* Duchess of Cleveland.

Lady Sussex undoubtedly incurred the implacable hatred of the
Duchess of Portsmouth for acting as go-between. The Duchess of
Cleveland wrote to her daughter from France, furious at her
behaviour, but the King supported Lady Sussex against her own
mother. Eventually, however, Lord Sussex insisted that his infatuated young wife should retire to his country estate, Hurst-
monceux Castle in Sussex. There for a time Lady Sussex pined for
the friend to whom she was passionately attached.

Even Courtin, skilled in petticoat diplomacy, found it difficult
to reconcile Louise and Hortense, though he later succeeded to
some extent. On one occasion his method was certainly unorthodox. He invited both ladies to sup with him at his house. When
he saw that they were in a convivial mood, he caused them to be
locked up in a closet together. The other guests waited in sus-
pense, anticipating the howls of rage, which would come to
them from the locked room. To their astonishment, however,
when the door was unlocked, Louise and Hortense came out hand-
in-hand and in their most sprightly fashion skipped down the
stairway.

The ambassador was present on 18th January 1677 when the
Duchess of Portsmouth was paying one of her rare calls on the
Duchesse Mazarin. Courtin must have been nervous lest some
ugly incident should mar the occasion. Then Nell Gwyn, accompanied by an intriguing, meddling woman named Lady Harvey,
a sister of Ralph Montagu, who hated the Duchess of Portsmouth,
made an appearance. Lady Harvey was celebrated for her wit,
though she was no real friend of Nell Gwyn's. Nell took the
opportunity of thanking the Duchesse Mazarin for sending her
compliments when her elder son had been recognized by
Charles II and created Earl of Burford. Forced compliments were
exchanged between the three mistresses and Lady Harvey. Courtin
reported later to Pomponne: "Everything passed off quite gaily
and with many civilities from one to the other, but I do not suppose that in all England it would be possible to get together three
people more obnoxious to one another." Everybody was greatly
relieved when Louise made her departure. Nell could restrain
herself no longer. She turned to the Ambassador with a bold,
merry look. "Why is it," she asked, "that the King of France does

John Wilmot second Earl of Rochester.
Drawn by D. Loggan in 1671

John Dryden, painted in about 1664 by
an unknown artist

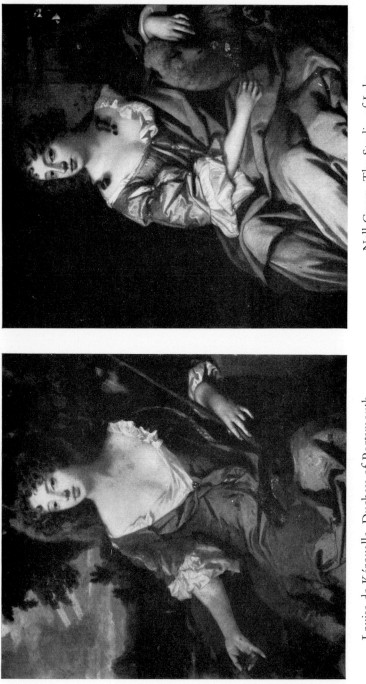

Nell Gwyn. The Studio of Lely

Louise de Kéroualle, Duchess of Portsmouth,
by Sir Peter Lely

not send presents to me, instead of to 'the weeping willow', who has just gone out? I promise you that he would get more profit by doing so. The King is a thousand times fonder of me than of her."

Courtin was beginning to enjoy himself, especially when the other ladies, tactfully wanting to change the subject, asked Mrs. Nelly if they could inspect her undergarments. Mrs. Nelly was only too ready to oblige them. The delighted ambassador reported to M. Pomponne, the Foreign Secretary: "Never in my life did I see such cleanliness, neatness and sumptuousness. I should speak," he added, "of certain other things which were shown to all of us, if Mr. de Lionne were still Foreign Secretary; but with you, Sir, I must be more grave and decorous."[5] Even Pomponne, however, was amused, for he wrote Courtin: "I am sure you forgot all your troubles when you were making Mistris Nesle raise those neat and magnificent petticoats of hers. . . ."[6] He found Courtin's accounts of the intrigues at the English court of some value and instructed him to continue them.

Both Nell Gwyn and the Duchess of Portsmouth gambled heavily at cards and sometimes lost large sums of money. A popular game at the court of Charles II was the French game of basset, introduced into England by the croupier Morin. On one occasion Nell Gwyn lost 1,400 guineas at basset to the Duchesse Mazarin, and on another occasion as much as 5,000 pounds.[7] Charles never encouraged his ladies to gamble at cards, for he invariably had to pay their losses. Hortense derived the greatest satisfaction when she won 8,000 pounds from the Duchess of Portsmouth at basset. This brilliant woman, who spoke six languages perfectly, was an extremely cunning player, for she sometimes gained the better of Charles II at basset. The privilege of acting as a *tallière*, or one that keeps the bank at basset, was much sought after. The King consequently made an edict that the privilege of acting as a *tallière* should be confined to principal cadets or sons of great families, for it was certain that such a *tallière* would soon possess considerable fortune.[8]

Another popular card game at the court of Charles II was L'Ombre, at which only three persons could play. This was the favourite pastime of the celebrated actor Cardonnel Goodman,

H

who was also a notorious gambler. He played the part of Alex-ander the Great in Nathaniel Lee's tragedy, *The Rival Queens*. Subsequently he became one of the many lovers of the Duchess of Cleveland, who took a fancy to him and maintained him at her own expense. In 1684—the year before Charles II died—gambling was still a passion at court, though the craze was for comette, which now exceeded basset in popularity.

During the spring (1677) the star of Hortense Mazarin was in the ascendant. At the opening of Parliament in February she appeared in a very conspicuous position, raised above all the other ladies behind the throne.[9] This must have been galling enough to the Duchess of Portsmouth, though Nell Gwyn would have made a ripe jest about it. Charles gave Hortense a pension of 4,000 pounds. Courtin assured Louvois on 25th February that he was on very friendly terms with the Duchesse Mazarin, and that she had no intention of intriguing with France's enemies.

If Hortense had been less unstable in temperament and less mercurial in her love life, it is probable that she would have retained her position at court as *maîtresse en titre*. During early 1677 the young handsome Prince of Monaco, who lived in a castle high above Monte Carlo, was in London. He had known Hortense in Savoy, and was known to be an ardent admirer. He could not disguise that he was desperately in love with her. Courtin wrote Louvois that the prince's profound melancholy made him doubtful whether his love would be successful.[10] When summer came, the prince was anxious to return to Monaco, because the English climate did not suit him, and he was suffering from a tertiary fever. In desperation he renewed his entreaties that Hortense should become his mistress. What Charles II would have described as Hortense's frailty of nature was no proof against the prince's insistence. Did he not write once to Minette that he was one of those bigots who regarded malice as a much greater sin than a poor frailty of nature? It was soon evident to the courtiers that the prince no longer sighed in vain. At first Charles took umbrage at her infidelity and revoked her pension. But it was not in his nature to harbour resentment for long. Within a few weeks he generously agreed to restore it. So, the Duchesse of Mazarin took the Prince of Monaco as her new lover, and the Duchess of Portsmouth was rid of a dangerous rival. Her position at Charles II's court was now assured for the remainder of his life, though Nell Gwyn continued to declare intermittent warfare on her. The courageous cockney was determined to challenge the supremacy of her detested rival whenever possible.

XI   *Her Kindness of Heart*

NELL GWYN had an extremely kind heart, and in the days of her prosperity she was always prepared to help others. She rarely interfered in political matters, but on one occasion, in June 1677, she interceded with some success for her friend George Villiers Duke of Buckingham when he had fallen foul of Charles II. Buckingham had argued with considerably ability in the House of Lords, quoting from a statute of Edward III that parliament should be dissolved rather than prorogued from month to month. He supported Lord Shaftesbury in his contention that, as there had been no session for over a year, it was virtually dissolved already. "Acts of Parliament," he said with ribald humour, "were not like women, the worse for being old." His motion, however, was defeated by a large majority, and Buckingham and three other peers, after refusing to apologize for ridiculing the censure of the Lords, were sent to the Tower of London.

Buckingham's character resembled in many ways that of Philip Duke of Wharton, whose tergiversations during the reign of King George I were later to baffle and fascinate his contemporaries. Both were notorious rakes, completely unstable and capable on occasions of making brilliant speeches. Buckingham was very dissolute. His mistress was the beautiful Anne Maria Brudenell Countess of Shrewsbury, whose husband he had badly wounded in a duel.* John Dryden's penetrating character sketch of Buckingham in his great satirical poem *Absalom and Achitophel* (1681) has never been surpassed. There he is depicted as Zimri:

---

* The duel was fought at Barn Elms on 16th January 1668. The Earl of Shrewsbury died two months later.

> A man so various, that he seem'd to be
> Not one, but all mankind's epitome:
> Stiff in opinions, always in the wrong;
> Was everything by starts, and nothing long;
> But, in the course of one revolving moon,
> Was chymist, fiddler, statesman and buffoon.
> Then all for women, panting, rhyming, drinking,
> Besides ten thousand freaks that died in thinking.

Nell had known him in the early days in 'The King's House', when Buckingham would loll in the pit with Etherege or another of his cronies. She later never stood any nonsense from him. The Duke of Bucks undoubtedly was a talented playwright, and when his play *The Rehearsal* was performed at 'The King's House' in December 1671 he had personally coached John Lacy in the part of Mr. Bayes, for he was eager that he should be familiar with the mannerisms of John Dryden. Lacy wore a suit of black velvet, since this was the poet laureate's favourite dress. In Buckingham's play *The Chances*, which is really a revised version of Beaumont and Fletcher's play, he alludes to Nell "dancing a jig" in the epilogue.

> The author dreads the strut and mien
> Of new prais'd poets, having often seen
> Some of his fellows, who have writ before,
> When Nell has danc'd her jig, steal to the door,
> Hear the pit clap and with conceit of that
> Swell, and believe themselves the Lord knows what.

Now when he was in trouble, Nell felt sorry for him, and concerted means with her friend Laurence Hyde, and various members of the 'merry gang', whereby His Grace of Buckingham could be freed from his irksome imprisonment. She used her influence on his behalf with her royal lover.

There is an unsigned and undated letter in the British Museum,[1] which reveals that Nell Gwyn was able to visit Buckingham in the Tower and to deliver a written message to him from the Earl of Middlesex (Lord Buckhurst).

> The best woman in the world brings you this paper, and, at this time, the discreetest. Pray, my Lord, resign your understanding and your interest wholly to her conduct. Mankind is to be redeemed by

Eve, with as much honour as the thing will admit of. Separate your concern from your fellow-prisoner [Lord Shaftesbury], then an expedient handsome enough, and secret enough to disengage yourself: obey, and you are certainly happy.

It is highly diverting that Nell should be referred to as "the discreetest", for she delighted her contemporaries by her indiscretions. Buckingham now wrote a letter to Charles II, in an atrocious hand, appealing to the King's sentiments, for they had known each other in boyhood and had later been companions in exile while Charles was in France. The King certainly found him an amusing companion but never really trusted him in state affairs. Buckingham wrote:

> I am so surprised with what Mrs. Nelly has told me, that I know not in the world what to say. . . . What you have been pleased to say to Mrs. Nelly is ten thousand times more than ever I can deserve. What has made this inclination more violent in mee, than perhaps it is in other people, is the honour I had of being bred up with your Majesty from a childe, for those affections are strongest in men, which begin in theyre youngest yeares. And therefore I beseech your Majesty to believe me when I say that I have ever loved you more than all the rest of mankind. . . . I wish that all the curses imaginable may fall upon mee, if I tell you a lye to free my life. . . .²

Buckingham's supplications made an impression on the King, for he was freed after a few days. Nell Gwyn proved a staunch friend to the duke in later days, when his health and fortunes were wrecked.

Buckingham was, like his gifted friend, a brilliant mimic. No doubt the two amused each other sometimes in Nell's house in Pall Mall, imitating the various politicians and their wives at Court: the Danbys; the Sunderlands; and others. Nell disliked Lord Danby, who was for some time in league with the Duchess of Portsmouth. When Danby refused to support her claims to become a countess, Mrs. Nelly, as she was known to her friends, was "at perfect defiance with him". Sir Robert Southwell wrote to James first Duke of Ormonde on 22nd September 1677: "The King looks on with great delight, which has been a fat prognostic unto some."³ Nell's clever imitation of the Lord Treasurer's wife, Lady Danby, a hard avaricious woman, appealed to his sense of humour. Bishop Burnet wrote that Lady Danby was more than half mad and forced her husband to pursue all her quarrels as well as his own.

Paul Barillon d'Amoncourt, Marquis de Branges, who succeeded Honoré de Courtin as French Ambassador in London in 1677, came of a legal family. He was extremely astute, and possessed an almost uncanny instinct for sensing which politicians could most easily be bribed. He was master in the art of corrupting men. Many prominent politicians were on Barillon's payroll, even the republican Algernon Sidney,[4] who received 500 pounds every parliamentary session from Louis XIV.

After 1676 James Duke of York became increasingly unpopular in England, mainly because he had openly acknowledged himself to be a Roman Catholic. Anthony Ashley Cooper first Earl of Shaftesbury wished to exclude James altogether from the throne and was bitterly opposed to the King and his brother. He encouraged James Duke of Monmouth, Charles II's illegitimate son by his Welsh mistress, Lucy Walter, in his pretensions that he was legitimate. He impudently told Charles II that, if only he would acknowledge his marriage to Mrs. Barlow★ (as Lucy Walter had been known during her later life), he would find witnesses to prove it. The King then said, "I'd rather see him hanged at Tyburn." Shaftesbury, a ruthless, ambitious man, realized that the protestant Duke of Monmouth was adored by the people. He wished to set him up as a puppet king, while he himself exercised real power.[5] Dryden in his *Absalom and Achitophel* described him with invective.

> A fiery soul which, working out its way,
> Fretted the pigmy body to decay,
> And o'er-informed the tenement of clay.†

The character of Monmouth had conflicting elements. He was handsome, brave, charming, superstitious, vain and easily imposed on. Astrologers soon discovered that His Grace of Monmouth had a pathetic faith in their predictions. Nell Gwyn knew him well and found him sympathetic. The feminine streak in Monmouth

★ Lucy Walter, who came of a good Pembrokeshire family, took the name of Barlow from some relations of her family.

† Shaftesbury was in constant pain, owing to an accident in his youth when the pole of his coach pierced his side.

would have appealed to her maternal instincts. Yet on one occasion she called him to his face "Prince Perkin". Monmouth retaliated by calling Nell ill-bred, and she then turned on him, aptly taunting him: "Was Mrs. Barlow better bred than I?" Monmouth, with his Celtic mysticism inherited from his Welsh mother, was a dreamer rather than a man of action. At the time of the Popish Terror in 1678, both the Duke of York and Monmouth were sent into temporary exile. The King, however, was very angry when he heard that Monmouth had later returned without permission. Although Charles still doted on his misguided son, he refused to see him, forbade him the court and ordered him once more to leave for Holland.

Even Nell Gwyn, despite her entreaties, could not influence Charles's determination. A contemporary account stated:

Nelly dus the Duck of Monmouth all the kindness shee can, but her interest is nothing. Nell Gwin begg'd hard of his Maj^{tie} to see him, telling him he was grown pale, wan, lean and long-visag'd merely because he was in disfavour; but the King bid her be quiet for he w^d not see him.

Possibly Monmouth thought that Nell's influence with the King was greater than it was, for he spent much time "shut up in her closet".[6] While the people in London drank toasts to their Protestant duke and lit bonfires in the streets, the King remained adamant. Even the office of Master of the Horse, formerly held by Monmouth, was now in commission. "He makes great court to Nelly," wrote Lady Sunderland to the Honourable Henry Sidney, English Ambassador in Holland.[7] Earlier, on 20th September 1678, Lord Chancellor Boyle had written to the Duke of Ormonde in Ireland that Nell Gwyn was very intimate with the Duke of Buckingham. "His present favour and allowance to have his lodgings in Madame Nelly's house, doth not a little contribute to the jealousies and dissatisfactions of the people,"[8] he wrote. Presumably Nelly wanted to show the Duke of Bucks that she was a constant friend.

It is related that Nell Gwyn did her utmost to relieve the financial distress of Samuel Butler;* author of the celebrated

* 1612–1680. Buried in St. Paul's Covent Garden and given a memorial in Westminster Abbey.

poem *Hudibras*. This was a favourite poem of Charles II, who used to carry a copy of the book with him and was fond of quoting from it. Though Nell endeavoured to influence Charles to offer Butler some gainful employment at court and persuaded her friend Buckingham to introduce him to William Wycherley, the author of *Hudibras* was stricken with poverty and died poor. Nell Gwyn took a lively interest in literature. As already mentioned, when her son was 10 years old in 1680, she appointed Thomas Otway, the tragic dramatist as his tutor. A scurrilous verse in the British Museum refers to this:

> Then for that cub, her son and heir,
> Let him remain in Otway's care. ,
> To make him (if that's possible to be)
> A viler Poet, and more dull than he.[9]

Otway was a jovial companion, but too fond of the bottle, being particularly partial to punch. One wonders whether Nell and her son's tutor ever drank this liquor together. Just before he died in squalor at the early age of 33, on 14th April 1685, Otway composed a song in which he eulogized punch. Contant D'Orville relates in the third part of *Les Nuits Anglaises ou Recueil* that Nell was generous to the playwright, Nathaniel Lee, and to Otway. In D'Orville's opinion, Nell's beauty was both "*mignonne* and *piquante*". Authors and dramatists hastened to dedicate their works to Nelly, a sure indication that she was a person of influence. In 1674, for instance, Thomas Duffet, dedicated his play, *The Spanish Rogue,* to her, writing in the adulatory language characteristic of that period that Nelly was so readily and frequently doing good, "as if doing good was not her nature, but her business". Mrs. Aphra Behn dedicated her play *The Feigned Courtezans,* produced at the Duke's Theatre in 1679 to Mrs. Ellen Gwyn. She has been criticized for the gross flattery in the dedication, but it may have been genuine. "You never appear," she wrote, "but you glad the hearts of all that have the happy fortune to see you, as if you were made on purpose to put the whole world in good humour." When thousands of people were made homeless in November 1682 by a devastating fire at Wapping, the King gave 2,000 pounds, and Madam Gwyn 100 pounds to relieve the suffering.

It is difficult to believe that Nell Gwyn was very religious by temperament, although towards the end of her short life she certainly came under the influence of Dr. Thomas Tenison, the erudite vicar of St. Martin-in-the-Fields, later Archbishop of Canterbury. She was a Protestant and supported that religion, if only to oppose the Duchess of Portsmouth, a rabid Papist. Rochester wrote in his poem 'A Panegyrick on Nelly':

> True to the Protestant interest and cause,
> True to th' Established Government and laws;
> The choice delight of the whole mobile,
> Scarce Monmouth's self is more belov'd than she.
> Was this the cause that did their quarrel move,
> That both are Rivals in the People's love?

As Charles II's mistress Nell always remained "the darling strumpet of the Crowd".

John Wilmot, second Earl of Rochester, sometimes refers to Nell Gwyn in his letters and various writings in such a benignant manner that one is tempted to doubt whether some of the lampoons written about her are really his work. As a lyric poet, this strange, complex, tempestuous man had a touch of genius. To the Victorians Rochester was a cynical debauchee and a wicked rake, but this is only partly the truth. He has been described with insight by an American critic John Harold Wilson as "one of the greatest sinners of a sinful age, also one of the finest and most daringly speculative minds of the age of reason".[10] With Rochester it is necessary to divorce the man from the artist. Of all the 'merry gang', who played their brief part at the court of Charles II, Rochester had the most original mind.

He was for ever experimenting. His constant infidelities as a husband were the means whereby he found real love for his wife. His sensual experiences formed a contrast to the spiritual love which he aspired to. So his tortured mind could conceive poetry of a poignant sensitivity and realism.

> Absent from thee I languish still,
> Then ask me not, when I return?
> The straying Fool, 'twill plainly kill,
> To wish all Day, all Night to Mourn

Dear from thine arms then let me flie,
   That my Fantastick Mind may prove,
The Torments it deserves to try,
   That tears my fix't Heart from my Love.

Nobody who reads his absorbing letters to his wife at Adder-bury in Oxfordshire can fail to understand that the young noble-man really loved his wife. "I doe seriously with all my heart wish myself with you, and am endeavouring every day to get away from this place, which I am so weary of that I may be said rather to languish [a favourite word] than live in it,"[11] he once wrote her.

Rochester* was a divided personality. His father had been a devoted adherent of Charles II, and his mother had come from solid Puritan stock. He was educated at Wadham College, Ox-ford, and, after receiving a lavish grant from the King, travelled for a while on the Continent, where he studied at the University of Padua. When he appeared at Charles II's court in 1664, he was renowned for his wild behaviour and success in seducing women. Anthony à Wood relates that "the Court not only debauched him, but made him an absolute Hobbist". Rochester seduced the heiress Elizabeth Malet, and married her. For this offence he languished in the Tower for six weeks. Later he served in the English fleet under Lord Sandwich and distinguished himself by his bravery. For a time he was in favour with Charles II, but not for long. Mrs. Jameson, in her memoirs of *The Beauties of the Court of Charles II*, suggests that Nell had formerly been Rochester's mistress, though there is no evidence of this. When the dark-eyed, lovely Elizabeth Barry, whom Rochester had trained for the stage with Nell Gwyn's help about 1673, gave Rochester a daughter, Nell criticized him for his lack of gener-osity and bowels towards the actress, who had not refused him the full enjoyment of her charms. This had its effect, for Rochester sent Elizabeth Barry a costly present.

An intimate friend of Rochester's was Henry Savile, a cultured wit and member of 'the merry gang'. A younger brother of Sir George Savile, later Marquess of Halifax, Henry Savile in

* 1647–1680.

appearance was corpulent and ruddy, while Rochester was tall, slim and handsome. Savile's entertaining letters addressed to the earl shed gleams of light on Charles's court. When Rochester was absent from Court or in disgrace in the country, his friend was in the habit of writing him the latest gossip. On 4th June 1678, he informed him of Lady Harvey's intrigue to try and supplant 'Mrs. Nelly' by making Mrs. Jenny Middleton Charles II's mistress. This lady was the same Jane Middleton, whom Honoré de Courtin had so admired. Lady Harvey (Elizabeth Montagu), wife of Sir Daniel Harvey, ranger in Richmond Park, belonged to the country or opposition party, which was opposed to the court. She has been described as "a woman of bold and enterprising spirit". An ardent intriguer, she sought to gain power over 'Charlemayne'* by supplying him with a new mistress. Nevertheless, Charles II was quite capable of choosing them for himself. In Savile's opinion, Mrs. Nelly was "too giddy to mistrust a false friend".

Savile wrote:

My Lady Harvey, who allwayes loves one civil plott more, is working body and soule to bring Mrs. Jenny Middleton into play. How dangerous a new one is to all old ones I need not tell you, but her ladyship, having little opportunity of seeing Charlemayne upon her owne account, wheedles poor Mrs. Nelly into supping twice or thrice a week at W. C. Chiffinch's carryeing her with her; soe that in good earnest this poor creature is betrayed by her Ladyship to pimp against herself. . . .[12]

At Nelly's candlelit supper parties Charles welcomed the opportunity of talking to members of the opposition or country party, as well as to those who supported him.

It is obvious that Savile and Rochester were anxious lest Lady Harvey's plot should succeed. Rochester's answer makes it clear that he bore no malice to Nelly, for he refers to her in a friendly way. "My advice to the lady," he wrote, "has ever been this, take your measures just contrary to your Rivals, live in peace with all the world, and easily with the King: Never be so illnatur'd to stir

* One of Charles II's nicknames.

up his anger against others, but let him forget the use of a passion, which is never to do you good: Cherish his love wherever it inclined...."[13] The greatest folly, he assured her, was to pretend to be jealous. Her wisest course was, "with body, head, heart", to contribute to his pleasure and comply with his desires. It is probable that Nell, after seven years as Charlemayne's mistress, was more confident of retaining his affection and trust than Rochester supposed.

During December 1677 a French troop of actors, who were bound for Nimeguen, were obliged, owing to contrary winds, to take refuge in England. They were invited to perform at Whitehall. Savile eagerly wrote to Rochester that it was a thousand pities they could not stay, "especially a young wench of fifteen, who has more beauty and sweetnesse than ever was seen upon the stage since a friend of ours [Nell Gwyn] left it". We do not hear whether Charles II showed any interest in the young French girl. If he had, it is certain that the Duchess of Portsmouth would have been jealous.

Whatever Rochester's feelings were towards Nell Gwyn, it is certain that he disliked the Duchess of Portsmouth. In August 1675 he was at his country seat, having just been involved in a very serious accident when he had been thrown from his horse. Savile informed him that he had incurred the deep resentment of the Duchess of Portsmouth. Later Rochester wrote bitter lampoons about the French favourite, particularly attacking her in 'The Busse' or 'The Royal Kisse' or 'Prorogation November 22nd 1675'. In his lampoon 'The Restoration' or 'The History of Insipids', Rochester denounces the King. Her Grace of Portsmouth was extremely unpopular because the anti-French and anti-Catholic sentiment in England was very acute. All sorts of wild rumours were bandied about in the coffee-houses; that she had transferred large amounts of money to France and that she was even taking the King there to live with her. A shrewd observer in London, the Venetian diplomat, Paolo Sarotti, wrote to the Doge and Senate on 29th November 1675: "The more politically minded dwell upon the quantity of gold which the King has given and which he lavishes daily upon his most favoured lady, who is a Frenchwoman."[14]

Rochester continued to attack Louise in his scurrilous verses, such as 'Portsmouth's Looking Glass'.

> Methinks I see you, newly risen
> From your embroider'd Bed and pissing,
> With studied mien and much grimace,
> Present yourself before your glass,
> To vanish and smooth o'er those graces,
> You rubb'd off in your Night Embraces. . . .

A letter from Buckingham to Rochester is significant, since it seems to suggest that one of Rochester's lampoons was the work of another. Buckingham wrote: "My noble friends at Court have now resolved as the most politick notions they can goe upon, to ly most abominably of your Lordship and mee in order to which they have brought in a new treasonable lampoone of which your Lordship is to be the author."[15]

In April 1677 Rochester wrote to Arthur Capel Earl of Essex,* informing him that he had been appointed a trustee in a certain matter which concerned Mrs. Nelly, requesting the Earl's favour. "My part is noe more but to advise her (as I would all I wish well to) by any means to bee oblig'd to Yr Excellence if they can, since there is noe where to bee found a better friend or worthyr patron."[16]

Like Buckingham, "the wicked Earl" was a brilliant mimic. After he had been exiled from court for offending the King in a bitter satire, he disguised himself as an Italian astrologer, 'Alexander Bendo', and many celebrated people visited Tower Hill to be cured of their ills and to learn some occult lore. 'Alexander Bendo's' advertisement, originally issued as a broadside circular, attracted the curious. It read: "They that will do me the favour to come to me, shall be sure from three o'clock in the afternoon, till eight at night, at my lodgings in Tower Street, next door to the sign of the Black Swan, at a goldsmith's house."

It is difficult, however, to excuse Rochester's vicious attack on John Dryden, for on one occasion he had the poet savagely assaulted as he returned home from Will's Coffee House. It is

---

* The Earl of Essex was later involved in the Rye House Plot and cut his throat in the Tower before his trial.

possible that he was envious of the dramatist's success. In September 1677 he again caused scandal by running naked along Woodstock Park with Mylord Lovelace and ten other men. This mad frolic deeply shocked Robert Harley,* who was inclined to be puritanical as a young man. Rochester himself explained the matter to Harry Savile in a letter: "We went into the river somewhat late in the year and had a frisk for forty yards in the meadow, to dry ourselves."[17]

Under the influence of Gilbert Burnet, later Bishop of Salisbury, Rochester repented of his ill-spent life, and, no longer a helpless victim in "doubt's boundless sea" like the lost traveller, found consolation as a convert to conventional Christianity. As he lay weak and emaciated in his lodge at Woodstock Park on a night in late June 1680, Rochester groped for his pen, and wrote to his friend Dr. Burnet a few lines:

My Most Honoured D[te] Burnet,
    My spirits and body decay so equally together that I shall write you a letter as weak as I am in person. I begin to value chuchmen above all men in the world and you above all Churchmen I know in it.[18]

Burnet in *Some Passages in the Life and Death of John, Earl of Rochester*, (1680), wrote eloquently about Rochester, who died at 34. "Like a Comet, he flashed across the stormy night of the seventeenth century, filling those who knew him with astonishment, leaving behind a memory that faded after many years." When she heard of his death, Nell Gwyn would have thought of Rochester in a magnanimous way, even if he had wronged her on occasions.

* Later First Earl of Oxford.

Nell Gwyn's Letters

IT is a great pity that Nell Gwyn was unable to write her own letters but was dependent on a secretary, for her letter to her friend Laurence Hyde, younger son of the Lord Chancellor Clarendon,* is very characteristic of her. Her sharp wit, her vulgarity, her frankness and her warmheartedness delight us. Charles II liked Laurence better than his brother Henry Lord Clarendon and called him 'Lory'. A story is told of them. Charles was in the habit of falling asleep if a sermon bored him, but on one occasion he was so pleased with a passage in a sermon by Laurence Hyde's Chaplain South that he turned to Hyde, saying, "Odsfish, Lory! Your Chaplain must be a Bishop, therefore put me in mind of him next vacancy."[1]

Bishop Burnet's opinion of Laurence Hyde was hardly flattering, though it may have been prejudiced. He tells us that he had a violent temper and drank excessively. "He has a very good pen, but speaks not gracefully," he wrote, "when he came into business, and rose to high posts, he grew both violent and insolent, but was thought by many an incorrupt man."[2] A brother-in-law of James Duke of York, he strongly advocated his cause during the Exclusion crisis (1679), although Hyde was a Protestant, like Nell Gwyn. She certainly was attached to him as a friend, and the likelihood is that Hyde was a more attractive personality than Burnet has depicted him.

Nell's letter to Lory Hyde was almost certainly written in June 1678, when he had been sent on a diplomatic mission to the Hague to negotiate the Peace of Nimeguen. The Treaty of Nimeguen was ratified on 10th August. Here is Nell's letter:

* Edward Hyde Earl of Clarendon died in exile 1674.

Hortense Mancini, later Duchesse Mazarin, telling her sister's
fortune. By Pierre Mignard

Nell Gwyn in the nude, by Sir Peter Lely

Nell Gwyn and her two sons, an engraving by Henri Gascar

Pray dear Mr. Hide forgive me for not writing to you before now, for the reason is I have been sick three months, and since I recovered I have had nothing to entertain you withal, nor have nothing now worth writing, but that I can hold no longer to let you know I never have been in any company without drinking your health, for I love you with all my soul.

The Pell Mell is now to me a dismal place since I have utterly lost Sir Carr Scrope never to be recovered again, for he told me he could not live always at this rate, and so, begun to be a little uncivil which I could not suffer from an ugly *beau garçon*.

Mrs. Knight's lady mother's dead and she has put up a scutcheon* no bigger than my Lady Green's scutcheon.

My Lord Rochester† is gone in the country. Mr. Savile‡ has got a misfortune, but is upon recover and is to marry an heiress, who I think won't have an ill time of it if he holds up his thumb. My Lord of Dorset appears worse in three months, for he drinks ale with Shadwell and Mr. Harris at the Duke's House all day long.

My Lord Burford remembers his service to you. My Lord Beau-clerk is going into France. We are a-going to sup with the King at Whitehall and Mylady Harvey. The King remembers his service to you. Now let us talk of state affairs, for we never carried things so cunningly as now, for we don't know whether we shall have peace or war, but I am for war, and for no other reason that you may come home.

I have a thousand merry conceits, but I can't make her§ write them, and therefore you must take the will for the deed. Good-bye —your most loving, obedient, faithful and humble servant,

E.G.[3]

The allusion to Sir Carr Scrope, who had been a friend of hers, is interesting. He was a crony of Charles II's, a courtier with a witty tongue, who wrote poetry. He had been created a baronet in 1668. He had earlier indulged in a violent quarrel with Catherine Sedley, the mistress of the Duke of York, for flinging the insult at her that she was "as mad as her mother and as vicious as

---

* Funeral brass.

† John Wilmot, second Earl.

‡ Henry Savile never married the heiress. He remained a bachelor. He later became Vice-Chamberlain of the Royal Household.

§ The amanuensis.

I

her father". Nell evidently also quarrelled with him. In alluding
to Sir Carr Scrope as an ugly *"beau garçon"*, she seems to be
familiar with an expression of Rochester's in one of his satirical
writings.

Mrs. Knight, a celebrated singer, was a friend and rival of Nell
Gwyn's. John Evelyn mentions in his diary* that Mrs. Knight and
other friends dined with him on one occasion. She subsequently
became a mistress of Charles II. According to Arthur Irwin
Dasent, Lady Green (Nell's amanuensis quaintly spells it 'Grin')
was Catherine Pegge, already referred to, who had been a mistress
of Charles II to while away the tedious days of exile in Bruges.
She was a neighbour and friend of Nell's in Pall Mall.

Lord Dorset was Nell's former lover. Owing to his influence,
Thomas Shadwell, the poet, was created poet laureate at the time
of the Revolution (1688), thus ousting Dryden. Joseph Harris was
a celebrated actor, who played Othello, Brutus, Cataline and
other rôles. My Lord Burford was her elder son, while my Lord
Beauclerk was her younger son. Lord Beauclerk, at the early age
of 8, died in September 1680 whilst staying in Paris.

It is interesting that Nell mentions to Laurence Hyde that she is
going to sup with the King and Mylady Harvey. It was on one of
these convivial evenings that Lady Harvey was intriguing to make
Jenny Middleton the King's mistress.

Nell's reference to the Dutch war is also curious and is very
typical of her irresponsible attitude towards politics. She favours
war, because Laurence Hyde would then be free to return home.
Her delightful phrase, "a thousand merry conceits", makes Nell
very vivid to us, and we can almost hear her gay prattle. She
always signed her letters or documents with her signature 'E.G.',
or occasionally Ellen Gwin.

There are other letters[4] of Nell Gwyn in the National Library
of Dublin. One is addressed to the great Duke of Ormonde,† at
that period Lord Lieutenant of Ireland, and concerns her Irish
pension. She is requesting Ormonde "to stand her freind" and to
use his influence to obtain for her this money. The letter was
written in 1682.

* 5th May 1659.
† James Butler first Duke, 1610–1688.

My Lord, [she wrote]

This is to beg a favor of your Grace, which I hope you will stand my freind in—I lately gott a freind of mine to advance me on my Irish Percon halfe a years payment for last Lady Day (wch all people have reced but me) and I drew bills upon Mr. Laurence Steele my agent for ye Pay^mt of ye money nott thinking but long before this, ye bills had been paid: but contrary to my Expectation I last night recd advice from him that ye bills are protested and he cannot receive any money without yo^e Graces positive order to ye payment for itt. . . . [5]

She goes on to remind the Duke that on a former occasion he had taken the trouble to ensure that she and Mrs. Forster received their pensions. Mrs. Forster was Rose, Nell's elder sister, to whom she was very much attached. Rose's first husband, the highwayman, John Cassells, had died in 1675, and later Rose married a man named Guy Forster. Some years before, Nell had persuaded Charles II to grant to herself and her sister certain monies that were raised in Ireland.

Earlier, Sir Robert Howard had corresponded with the Duke of Ormonde on Nell's behalf in an attempt to obtain money due to her from a grant of Irish property made by the King. Ormonde's influence was sought to help her cause in the Irish Court of Claims.[6] Nell had known Howard well during her career at 'The King's House', when she had acted in at least two of his plays. She was given the part of Samira in *The Surprisal* and Donna Maria in *The Great Favourite* or *The Duke of Lerma*. At this period Howard was secretary to the Treasury and had succeeded Sir George Downing in this post.

Ormonde, when replying to Sir Robert, 20th November 1677, suggested that Nell's pension should be put on the Establishment, until prior rights terminated. "Be pleased to let her know all this, and that I am her most obedient servant," he wrote.[7]

Somehow the warmth of Nell's nature peeps through the dull legal phrases of these letters. Sir Robert wrote to the Duke

Mrs. Nelly has commanded me to present her among your true servants and does think herself so much obliged to Your Excellency, that unless within a little time you command her something that she may serve you in, she swears she will pick a quarrel with you, for she vows she loves you entirely.[8]

The Howard-Ormonde correspondence continued for almost two years. On one occasion Sir Joseph Williamson, Secretary of State, who was not entirely admitted into Charles II's confidence concerning this transaction, wrote to Ormonde about the Dungannon estates in Ireland. The King also wished Nell to have this property. "Sir Robert Howard," he wrote, "is directed to give you a more particular account of His Majesty's mind and intentions in all that matter. All I know is that His Majesty told me it was a concern of his own, and in a certain sense for himself." The King wanted to grant the estates in Dundalk and Carlingford, if they were held to be in his gift, to Sir Robert Howard and his heirs. It is evident that Howard was merely acting as a Trustee for Nell Gwyn and her son, the Earl of Burford.

The Earl of Arran, Ormonde's son, wrote to his father on 16th March 1678: "Mrs. Gwyn sent for me the other day and desired my advice concerning money she should receive out of Ireland. Mr. Mulys, one of your servants, is her agent in the matter."

Evidently the Duke of Ormonde used his immense influence in a helpful way on Nell's behalf, for Howard wrote during November 1679, informing the Duke that her agent named Melish had necessarily been replaced by a new agent, and that Mrs. Nelly "presents you with her real acknowledgments for all your favours, and protests she would write in her own hand but her wild characters she says would distract you." A delightful touch, which suggests that Nell was capable of writing a few words, if she so chose. Howard added: "This, my Lord, was her own natural notion when I showed her your Grace's kind return upon the King's letter."[9]

She wrote, on 26th November 1682, to the Lord Arran, asking him "to stand my friend", regarding the matter of the arrears of her pension in Ireland. "My agent is Mr. Laurence Steele," she wrote to him, "to whom I have sent this letter to deliver to your lordship." It is evident that Nell is worried about her financial affairs. She was always too generous to others.

In a later letter* to the Duke of Ormonde, she reveals her real kindness of heart. She is using her influence to obtain for a Mr.

* 29th February 1684.

Clare some command in the army. It would seem that Mr. Clare held the post of tutor for almost three years in Nell Gwyn's household.

> I forgott yesterday [she wrote to him] to speak to you about Mr. Clare, wch makes me now trouble you with this letter, praying your Grace to give him some command in the army of Ireland. I have spoke to the King for him and the King said he would speak to your Grace, but least he might forgett it, he bad me do it. The King believes very well of Mr. Clare and would be well satisfied that he were provided for . . . for now that My Lord Duke of St. Albans is going into France, I have taken a French Governor in Mr. Clare's roome. . . .[10]

She signs her letter "Yr. Grace's most humble Servt. E. Gwyne." No record exists that Nell ever visited Ireland.

Another letter of Nell Gwyn's was written on 14th April 1684 from Burford House, Windsor, which was presented to her by Charles II. It is an intimate letter, which clearly shows that Nell was now acutely embarrassed by pecuniary difficulties. Nell dictated the letter to her secretary, to be delivered to "Madame Jennings, over against the Tub Tavern in Jermyn Street". Madame Jennings was almost certainly the mother of two famous daughters, Frances and Sarah, who subsequently became Duchess of Tyrconnel and Duchess of Marlborough. The letter reads:

> Madam—I have received your letter, and I desire you would speak to my Lady Williams to send me the gold stuff and a note with it, because I must sign it, ye next day of Mr. Trant; pray tell her ladyship that I will send her a note of what quantity of things I'll have bought, if her ladyship will put herself to ye trouble to putt them; when they are bought I will sign a note for her to be paid. Pray, Madam, let ye man go on with my sedan, and sent Potevine and Mr. Coker down to me for I want them both. The bill is very dear to boil the plate but necessity hath no law.
>
> I am afraid Madam you have forgot my mantle, which you were to line with musk colour satin, and all my other things, for you send me no patterns nor answer. Monsieur Lainey is going away. Pray send me word about your son Griffin, for His Majesty is mighty well pleased that he will go along with my Lord Duke. I am afraid you are so much taken up with your own house that you forget my

business. My service to dear Lord Kildare, and tell him I love him with all my heart. Pray, Madam, see that Potevine brings now all my things with him; my Lord Duke's* bed etc. if he hath not made them all up, he may do that here, for if I do not get my things out of his hands now, I shall not have them until this time twelvemonth.

The Duke brought me down with him my crochet of diamonds; and I love it the better because he brought it. Mr. Lumley and everybody else will tell you that it is the finest thing that ever was seen. Good Madam, speak to Mr. Beaver to come down too, that I may bespeak a ring for the Duke of Grafton† before he goes into France.

I have continued extreme ill ever since you left me, and I am so still. I have sent to London for a doctor. I believe I shall die. My service to the Duchess of Norfolk, and tell her, I am as sick as her grace, but do not know what I ail, although she does, which I am overjoyed that she does with her great belly.

Pray tell my Lady Williams that the King's mistresses are accounted ill paymasters, but she shall have her money the next day after I have the stuff.

Here is a sad slaughter at Windsor, the young men taking their leaves and going to France, and although they are none of my lovers, yet I am loath to part with the men. Mrs. Jennings, I love you with all my heart and so good-bye! E.G.

Lady Williams, referred to in the letter, was the widow of a Dorsetshire baronet, a former mistress of the Duke of York, and had formerly lived in fashionable St. James's Square. Potevin was an upholsterer; while Beaver was a jeweller. "Dear Lord Kildare" was the husband of one of Charles II's multitudinous mistresses.

Mary Mordaunt, Duchess of Norfolk, daughter of Henry second Earl of Peterborough, was a lady of immoral character. Nell's tart comment about her is of interest, because the Duchess of Norfolk was involved in 1692 in a celebrated divorce case for her guilty intimacy with Sir John Germain. Although Nell Gwyn had been dead for five years, her evidence was allowed during the State Trial.

An important member of Nell's household was Fleetwood Sheppard,‡ a typical Restoration courtier, who dabbled in poetry.

* Duke of St. Albans.
† Charles II's son by Lady Castlemaine.
‡ 1634–1698. Knighted in 1694.

He was fortunate in acquiring Lord Buckhurst, Nell's early lover, as his patron, and Sheppard accompanied Buckhurst when he visited Henry Savile, the English Ambassador in Paris in 1681. Sheppard was reputed to be an atheist, and to be too partial to the bottle and to whoring. It was owing to Buckhurst that Nell first became acquainted with Sheppard, and she appointed him her steward after the birth of her elder son. He was also responsible for managing her financial affairs. For these services, and for acting as a tutor to Charles Earl of Burford, he was irregularly paid 200 pounds per annum. During October 1678 Nell Gwyn and Sheppard visited Cambridge, where they were entertained by the Vice-Chancellor and proctors of that university. On this occasion Nell was delighted to have verses presented to her. Fleetwood Sheppard was a patron of Matthew Prior.

It is an illusion to imagine that Nell Gwyn's life constantly remained untroubled and carefree. From 1680 onwards she was to experience physical pain and illness and, despite her buoyant spirits, to be harassed by debts. The sudden death of her younger son, James Lord Beauclerk, at the early age of 8 in Paris (1680) grieved her deeply. There was always a naïve quality in Nelly, and she was wounded by the incessant intrigues at Court and by the insincerity of the courtiers. She was a poor judge of character, and she relied on Charles to tell her who her real friends were and who were false.

Nell was 30 in 1680, older in the Restoration era than it would seem today. One of the misfortunes of advancing age is to lose one's friends through death. Nell had never forgotten her early friends of the theatre. John Lacy, who had been her lover and taught her how to dance, died at his house near Cradle Alley in Drury Lane in September 1681. Two years later there died Charles Hart, to whom she owed her training as an actress. They had triumphed together so often in the leading rôles at the King's House. He was buried 20th August 1683 at Stanmore Magna, Middlesex, where he had a country house. A contemporary record says: "That worthy and famous actor Mr. Charles Hart ... departed this life Thursday August 18th, 1683."[11] In his dedication to *Fatal Love* or the *Forc'd Inconstancy* (1680), addressed to Sir Robert Owen, Elkana Settle wrote:

The Theatre Royal was once all Harmony. . . . But, oh, that their oracle should be quite silent! . . . that the best tragedies of the English Stage have received that lustre from Mr. Hart's performance, that he has left such an impression behind him, that no less than the interval of an age can make them appear agen with half their majesty, from any second Hand (and when he leaves the stage, the Reign of Tragedy expires).

Then in 1684 there died the gentle actor Michael Mohun, who had sometimes been a peacemaker in the frequent disputes between the players. Gout-stricken, feeble and old, Mohun struggled to maintain a family of five on his meagre earnings. He appealed to the King, and Charles did not forget in his need the actor who had given him pleasure on the stage, nor the gallant cavalier who had fought for his father in the Civil War. He died in a house in Brownlow Street, now named Betterton Street, near the theatre in 1684.[12] By 1683 Thomas Killigrew, "Father of Drury Lane", to whom Nell owed so much, was also dead.

XIII   *Nell Gwyn in the Country*

IT is well known that Charles II was most at ease at New-market, where he used to go a-hawking in the mornings and to cock-matches in the afternoons, if there happened to be no horse-matches. He often amused himself during the evenings attending the simple plays, usually acted in barns and sometimes by Bartholomew Fair comedians. He was a superb horseman and often rode himself in the races. When in Newmarket, Charles stayed at the old palace, until it was burnt down owing to the carelessness of a groom, who set fire to a haystack, during Charles II's visit in March 1683. Nell Gwyn often accompanied Charles on his visits to Newmarket. He bought for his mistress a house adjoining the palace, where he often came to see her. Local tradition relates that there was an underground passage between the palace and Nell's house.[1] Nell enlivened Charles's stay by her frolics, on one occasion wearing a horseman's coat, as if she hankered for the theatre. She once had a nasty tumble from her horse, for she was by no means an experienced rider.

There is an authentic story about Nelly and Charles II together at Newmarket, which is very entertaining. On one occasion, at the end of September 1681, a pompous Whig Alderman named Wright presented a petition to the King as he was walking in the country. "The King walking in ye fields met Nell Gwynne and Nell cal'd to him, 'Charles, I hope I shall have your company at night, shall I not?' " Alderman Wright, who was hostile to the King, was deeply shocked. He told his friends that he had often heard bad things of the King, but now his own eyes had seen it.[2]

After the discovery of the Rye House Plot (1683), which was an attempt to assassinate Charles II and the Duke of York as they returned to London from Newmarket, the King lost his enthusiasm

for this place. He planned the building of a new Palace at
Winchester, situated as it is in beautiful countryside. The palace
was to be designed by Sir Christopher Wren, and it was intended
that it should rival Versailles in all its splendour. In August 1684
Charles was anxious to make a visit of inspection to see how the
building was progressing, and the royal party included Nell Gwyn
and the Duchess of Portsmouth. It was the duty of a Court official
known as the 'harbinger' to arrange lodgings for the various
members of the Court. Unfortunately he wished to assign the
prebendal house of Thomas Ken, who had recently been appointed
a court chaplain, as the lodging for Nell Gwyn. It is probable that
the 'harbinger' supposed that Ken, to gain the royal favour, would
not allow his scruples to prevent him offering hospitality to Nelly.
But he did not know Thomas Ken. The fiery little man was very
angry. "A woman of ill-repute," he complained, "ought not to be
endured in the house of a clergyman, least of all in that of the
King's Chaplain."[3] Nell's choice vocabulary of swear words
would have amused Charles II when she heard of the insult.

It is related that Ken gave instructions to the builders that his
house should be repaired and that it should be unroofed. The
dean, Dr. Meggot, however, proved more subservient than the
prebendary. He immediately arranged that a room should be built
for her at the south end of the deanery, which was known by her
name for many years. Later Nell stayed at Avington, three miles
away, the country seat of Lady Shrewsbury, the Duke of Buckingham's mistress.

Unlike his brother, the Duke of York, the King very seldom
harboured resentment for long. A shrewd judge of character, he
always respected Ken's fearless honesty. When his name was
mentioned as a suitable candidate for a bishopric, Charles exclaimed: "Odsfish! Who *should* have Bath and Wells but the little
black fellow who would not give poor Nelly a lodging."[4]

On one occasion Nell Gwyn was robbed of ten guineas by a
highwayman, who waylaid her coach on a lonely stretch of the
road over Bagshot Heath. It is related that, with a laugh and a
grimace, Nell gave the fellow the money, since she had been
amused when he said, "I hope, madam, you will give me something for myself after I have took all you have away?"[5]

Very different was the haughty reaction of Louise de Kéroualle Duchess of Portsmouth, when she was robbed by a celebrated highwayman named 'Old Mobb' on the old Portsmouth Road. This robber was in league with the landlord of 'The Golden Farmer', a lonely inn on the Bagshot road. Louise was in her coach, attended by a small retinue. When 'Old Mobb' demanded her money, the French favourite stared icily at him, saying, "Do you know who you are addressing, you rascal?" "Yes, madam," replied Mobb with great composure. "Indeed I do, I know you to be the greatest whore in the kingdom and that you are maintained at the public charge. I know that all the courtiers depend upon your smiles and that the King himself is your slave. But what of that? A gentleman collector is a greater man on the road and much more absolute than His Majesty is at Court." Louise, no doubt furious, told 'Old Mobb' that he was an insolent fellow and warned him, in her French accent, that he would be sure to suffer for this affront. "Madam," answered 'Old Mobb', "that haughty French spirit will do you no good here. . . . Your money is English and a proof of English folly. I would have you know that I am king here. And I have also a whore of my own to keep on the public's contributions, just the same as King Charles has. . . ."⁶

Despite her loss of looks towards the end of the reign of Charles II, the Duchess of Portsmouth maintained her ascendancy and influence. When the new Moroccan Ambassador, named Nahed Hamet, was received at court in January 1682, it was the Duchess of Portsmouth who queened it in her luxurious apartments, providing a great banquet of sweetmeats and other delicacies. Nelly was present on this important occasion, and Evelyn naturally cannot refrain from his usual sneer. He mentions in his diary

that the Ambassador and his retinue behav'd themselves with extraordinary moderation and modesty, then plac'd aboute a long table, a lady between two Moores, and amongst these were the King's natural children, Lady Lichfield and Sussex, the Dutchess of Portsmouth, Nelly, etc. concubines and catell of that sort, as splendid as jewells and excesse of bravery could make them. . . .⁷

Charlotte, Countess of Lichfield, a daughter of Barbara Duchess
of Cleveland, was as virtuous as her mother was depraved. Evelyn
tells us that the ambassador and his entourage drank a little milk
and water, but no wine. The ambassador was fond of the theatre,
where he "could not forbear laughing", though he attempted to
restrain it. His present to the King consisted of "two lions and
thirty ostridges", whereupon Charles laughed and said in his witty
way that he knew nothing more proper to send by way of return
than a flock of geese.[8] The diplomat was shrewd enough to take
his leave of the Duchess of Portsmouth later in July, with the
prayer that God would bless her and the prince, her son, the little
Duke of Richmond.

It must not be supposed that Queen Catherine of Braganza
completely lacked influence at her husband's court. Charles
always treated her with respect, and it was his habit to rebuke his
mistresses if they slighted the Queen. On one occasion, after the
Rye House Plot, when the Duke of Monmouth's life was in
jeopardy, for he was deeply involved, Catherine successfully
interceded for the misguided young man with her husband. Like
Nell Gwyn, she was fond of Monmouth. In his middle age Charles
found Catherine a devoted companion. Lady Sunderland, writing
to a friend in 1680, refers to "the King and Queen, who is now a
mistress, the passion her spouse has for her is so great. . . ." If Lady
Sunderland intended to write ironically, there was nevertheless
some truth in it. Occasionally Catherine's Latin temper flared, for
instance during April 1683 at Windsor, when she was together
with her husband. High words passed between the royal couple,
when the King remarked that the Queen enjoyed more privileges
regarding her servants than any of her predecessors. The Queen
immediately retorted that her mother-in-law Queen Henrietta
Maria had possessed many more privileges, "but today the mistresses govern all". In his peculiar way Charles loved Nelly,
Louise and the Queen and needed them all. No more complex
man has ever sat on the throne of England.

Nell Gwyn had always longed for a country home of her own,
and it was in 1681 that Charles II assigned by royal warrant
Burford House, a redbrick house in Windsor to her. Charles II
settled Burford House on Nell Gwyn in trust for their son, Charles

Beauclerk Earl of Burford. The Guildhall at Windsor possesses a large print of Kyp's entitled "A Prospect of the House at Windsor Belonging to His Grace Charles Beauclerc Duke of St. Albans, Earl of Burford and Baron of Headington. Captain of the Honbl. Band of Gentlemen Pensioners, Marshall and Surveyor of the Hawkes to His Maj'tie (William III)* and one of the gentlemen of his Maj'tie's Bed Chamber." If this print dates from 1709, it was the work of Kyp during the reign of Queen Anne.

Windsor has more intimate associations with Nell Gwyn than any place other than London. Burford House, named after her elder son, was situated on the site now adjacent to the Queen's mews, so Charles could easily visit Nelly on his frequent visits to Windsor Castle from 1680 onwards. Antonio Verrio, the Italian artist, who had done invaluable decorative work when the castle was restored, was ordered by the King to paint the staircases in Burford House.[9] They were decorated with "stories of Ovid". Potevine, Nell's upholsterer in Pall Mall, supplied the furniture. Henceforward she was to enjoy halcyon summer days at Windsor, delighting in the companionship of Charles II, especially when her rival Her Grace of Portsmouth happened, on account of ill health, to be drinking the waters of Bourbon in France. So it was at the beginning of March 1682, when Louise returned to her native country for a few months to enjoy the excessive favours heaped on her by Louis XIV. With a sense of triumph she was now granted the privilege to sit on a tabouret when she went to pay her respects to the Queen.

Nell delighted in the sylvan beauty of Windsor, in her day an enchanting little red-roofed town, with its fascinating streets below the castle walls, such as Priest Street (now St. Albans Street) and Church Street. Nell would have been familiar with Pescod (Peascod) Street, an ancient street, which is mentioned in local records during the reign of Henry III. Its name is intriguing. Perhaps there originally stood a priest's croft or house in the neighbourhood, or there may have been a pea garden. A tradition says that Nell also occupied a house in Church Street—now an antique business—but it rests on very slender evidence. The date of this house is 1640—ten years before she was born, so it is just

* William III died in 1702.

possible that she may later have stayed here for a day or two on one of her visits to Windsor. A tunnel in the cellar is reputed to lead to Windsor Castle. It is also related that she planted an avenue of lime trees at Kingswick in Sunninghill, possibly to commemorate some festive occasion.

Later, Princess Anne of Denmark and her husband Prince George, who was very fond of Windsor, after Nell Gwyn's death in November 1687 rented Burford House for some time from the Duke of St. Albans, paying 260 pounds a year. When the infant Prince of Wales* was two months old, a contemporary records that "he was removed from Richmond to Windsor, where he is lodged in the Princess of Denmark's house (which was Mrs. Ellen Gwyn's) and is well recovered of his late indisposition to the joy of the whole Court and the Kingdom."[11] If the Prince of Wales stayed at Burford House it is unlikely to have been for more than a night or two. Its later history is of considerable interest. George III eventually bought Burford House from the third Duke of St. Albans in 1777 and renamed it Lower Lodge.[11] On his death it passed to Queen Charlotte, who bequeathed it in her will to her youngest daughter, Princess Sophia. Princess Charlotte, the daughter of George IV, is known to have stayed there. Today it bears no resemblance to Nell Gwyn's home, though it is still used to provide accommodation for the Royal Household. It reverted to its original name of Burford House.

Nell was certainly attached to its lovely gardens and regarded them with pride. It had an orangery and bowling alleys covering many acres. When the first regular stage-coach service between Windsor and London was started in 1673, the watermen complained bitterly that it was ruining their livelihood.

Nell owned other property in Windsor besides Burford House. Some ancient documents[12] in the Dean's Cloister, Windsor Castle show that, on 11th December 1684, a lease of some property in Priest Street (now St. Albans Street) was granted "to Ellenor Gwinn of the Parish of St. Martin-in-the-Fields, Middlesex". The property included a bankside garden and an adjoining stable. About two acres, "in a place there called the Old Hawes

---

* Prince James Francis Edward, later known as King James the Third, or 'The Pretender' to his enemies.

between the King's garden there on the north part, and the garden of sundry persons on the west and south parts and the little park of Windsor", was also leased to her. Nell's signature 'E.G.' can clearly be distinguished on this document. The witnesses included Gregory Hascard, Dean of Windsor, and Mr. J. Clare, possibly the same gentleman on whose behalf Nell had earlier written to the Duke of Ormonde. Another witness was Robert Young, who had been headmaster of Eton and a chaplain to Prince Rupert.

This strange rugged character, with a touch of genius and a passion for science,* was in his later life Constable of Windsor Castle. He much preferred country life in Berkshire to the court of his cousin Charles II. He genuinely liked Nell Gwyn, and admired her honesty, contrasting it with the monstrous flattery of the courtiers at Whitehall. Prince Rupert's mistress Peg Hughes, the former actress, was now living in a house at Hammersmith. Before the prince died in London (1682), he gave his mistress a marvellous pearl necklace.† When her former colleague wished to sell it, Nell was very eager to acquire this heirloom and paid as much as 4,250 pounds for it. When dying, Prince Rupert was reported to have sent his garter to the King, requesting that it, together with the hand of his daughter (by Peg Hughes), might be bestowed on Lord Burford.[13] Charles never complied with his cousin's wish.

Charles II always behaved generously to Nell Gwyn. In 1681 he granted to her the lease of some land in Bestwood Park,‡ which lay within the borders of Sherwood Forest in Nottinghamshire. It was at Bestwood Lodge in Sherwood Forest that Richard III heard of the approach of the invading force of Henry Richmond. There is no record that Nell Gwyn ever visited Nottinghamshire, though a curious legend exists that she was promised by Charles II as large a slice of Sherwood Forest as she could ride round before breakfast. The leases[14] relating to Bestwood Park described Nell as "Lady Elinor Gwynne of the parish of St. Martin-in-the-Fields in the County of Middlesex".

* He was a founder member of the Royal Society.
† These pearls had once belonged to Elizabeth, Queen of Bohemia, ancestress of Queen Elizabeth II.
‡ King Edward III was fond of visiting and hunting in Bestwood Park.

When Nell was later embarrassed by financial troubles, she was forced to mortgage Bestwood Park to Sir John Musters. However, there is a later entry in the Secret Services Expenses accounts,[15] which reveals that, in 1685, after James II had ascended the throne, he behaved with magnanimity to his brother's mistress. He was probably aware that she had called him 'dismal Jimmie', but he did not allow it to rankle. Sir Stephen Fox was paid in full the large amount of £3,744 2s 6d for redeeming the mortgage on Bestwood Park. The property was again settled upon Mrs. Ellen Gwyn for life, and after her death it was proposed to settle it upon the Duke of St. Albans and his male issue, with the reversion in the Crown. She kept her account at Child's Bank, the oldest bank* in the country, and signed receipts with her initials 'E. G.' Among their interesting archives are several letters concerning the financial affairs of Mrs. Ellen Gwyn. There is a hurried note from one of her servants, James Booth, written almost certainly in 1684, which seems to suggest that Nell was in financial difficulties and was even obliged to pawn her jewels. Here is the note:

Jackson,†
　　Madam Gwyn desires you will come to her today for her jewells.

Y^{or} Servt J. Booth.

Nell Gwyn's enjoyment of country sports, particularly of horse races was appreciated by Charles II, who was much attached to Windsor. There in his later life, when he longed for peace from the turmoil of Whitehall, he could find it amid the water-meadows and willows, fishing its sluggish streams, or buck hunting in Windsor Forest. Nell was an influence in the land, and politicians and friends like handsome Henry Sidney‡ were always careful to visit 'Mrs. Nelly' at Burford House when they came to Windsor. The King gave Nell's son Charles Lord Burford the reversion of the hereditary office§ of Grand Falconer of England, and it must have pleased her that her son, at 14, would have the

* It was taken over by Messrs. Glyn Mills in 1924.
† An official of Childs Bank.
‡ Later Earl of Romney.
§ Sir Allen Apsley formerly held this office until his death in 1683.

responsibility of looking after the King's hawks. We can be sure that 'Mrs. Nelly' sometimes went a-hawking. She loved to ride amidst the cool forest glades.

Nell Gwyn was not of a jealous disposition, but it was galling for her to watch the progress of her rival Louise's only son, Charles Duke of Richmond. One can imagine her annoyance when the boy duke was, at the age of 4, granted by his father a perpetual charge on every ton of coal exported from the Tyne and consumed in England. In the Calendar of Domestic Papers during August 1680 there is a newsletter to Sir Francis Radcliffe of Dilston, which relates that Her Grace of Portsmouth had obtained a promise from the King that her son should be installed K.G., instead of Lord Ossory, the Duke of Ormonde's heir. Nor would Nell have been pleased when the City of York, during the spring of 1683, chose the Duke of Richmond, now 11, as their high steward. In the early days of her liaison with the King, Louise had even dared to hope that the Queen, since she was delicate, might die, so that the King could be free to marry her. Her sly eyes had gleamed with ambition. Then her Richmond might be acknowledged as heir to the throne. But the King had been loyal to the legitimate succession, and by 1682 it was clear that the Duke of York would succeed him eventually to the throne.

John Evelyn considered in 1684 that both the Duke of St. Albans and the Duke of Richmond "were pretty boys". "What ye Dukes of Richmond and St. Albans will prove, their youth does not yet discover," he wrote.* On Easter Day 1684 the King, accompanied by his three tall natural sons, the Dukes of Northumberland,† Richmond and St. Albans, took his communion at Whitehall, kneeling before the altar while he made his offering.

The Yorkshire squire Sir John Reresby, a staunch supporter of the King, relates in his memoirs that the Duchess of Portsmouth could be gracious enough if she chose. When he was at Windsor in June (1684), she was very kind to his wife and daughter. After inviting them to dine with her, she told Reresby that whenever he came to Windsor he should make her table his own.

---

* 24th October 1684.

† George Fitzroy, first Duke of Northumberland. Evelyn considered that he was the most promising of all King Charles's natural children.

Three years before a lively incident had occurred at Oxford, which again reveals the ancient rivalry between Nell and Louise. It was March 1681, a period of great discontent, when people even talked of civil war, so bitter was the feud between the Whigs, under Lord Shaftesbury, and the Tories, who supported the King. Charles was anxious that Parliament should be convened in Oxford, though this move was opposed by the Whigs. Oxford seethed with excitement. Armed bands of ruffians patrolled the streets shouting anti-Popish slogans. When a gilded coach made its cumbrous way through the streets the people jeered, thinking no doubt that it contained the detested 'Mrs. Carwell'. Just when the situation was beginning to look really ugly, Nell Gwyn put her head out of the window of the coach, and, to the delight of the people, cried: "Pray, good people, be civil. I am the Protestant whore." Perhaps this authentic story about Nell is more familiar than any of the others, yet it bears repetition.

Nell might mockingly refer to herself as 'the Protestant whore', yet she always remained faithful to her 'Charles III'. Her royal lover, too, far from "treating her with the lewdness of a prostitute", as Bishop Burnet falsely observed, learnt to trust her as a valued friend. It may be wondered why Charles never ennobled her, but she came of very humble stock. The barrier between people of noble birth and commoners was very wide in those times. There are indications, however, that Charles II had intended to create her Countess of Greenwich, but death intervened before he could do so.

There is a strong tradition that the Royal Hospital at Chelsea for aged and disabled soldiers owed its origin to the kindness of Nell Gwyn. Once having achieved a position of influence, she was known in her own day for the compassionate interest she took in others less fortunate than herself. It is more than possible that Nell inspired the foundation of this great hospital, but there is really no documentary evidence to connect her with it. Thomas Faulkner wrote:[16] "The anonymous author of the *Life of Eleanour Gwynn* (1742) states that it was at her instigation that this noble charity was established." "Another act of generosity," he says, "which raised the character of this lady above every other courtezan of these or any other times, was her solicitude to effect the institution of Chelsea Hospital." According to this story, which may be true, Nell was abroad one day in her coach when a poor man came to the coach door soliciting alms. He related to the sympathetic Nell a doleful story how he had been wounded during the Civil Wars whilst defending the cause of Charles I. Nell's generous heart overflowed with pity for the wretched man, and she at once reflected on the monstrous ingratitude of the Government in allowing the suffering of those, who had so valiantly served their country. She immediately hurried to Charles II to plead their cause, imploring him to allow some project to be proposed whereby those who had done this service should not, owing to old age, grievous wounds, or other infirmities, end their days oppressed with want or repining against fortune. There is the delightful story that Nell when she first saw Sir Christopher Wren's plan for building the Royal Hospital, tore her handkerchief into strips and made a hollow square with them. In such a characteristic way did she induce Charles II to double the size of the designed building.[17]

There is another anecdote,* which also rests on very dubious authority. When the garrison was withdrawn from Tangiers, there were many old and infirm persons among them. Consequently it was proposed to build a hospital for them. After the King had been approached to supply a piece of land for the site, he agreed to offer the ground on which St. James's College stood. Then, recollecting himself, he said, "Odsfish! 'Tis true I have already given that land to Nell here." Whereupon Nell Gwyn, who was conveniently present, said, "Have you so, Charles? Then I will return it to you again for this purpose." So the hospital was built. The foundation stone of the Royal Hospital was laid by Charles II in the spring (1682), consequently this story does not seem at all convincing. The Tangier garrison was withdrawn in 1683, owing to the stupid refusal of Parliament to vote money for its support.

John Evelyn was keenly interested in the proposal to build the Royal Hospital, but he never mentions Nell Gwyn in this connection. Evelyn, however, had a poor opinion of Nell, as has been already mentioned. In his diary he frequently records the interest

* Also mentioned in Thomas Faulkner's book on Chelsea.

of Sir Stephen Fox,* a Lord Commissioner of the Treasury, in this
noble venture. Sir Stephen was a public spirited man, who had
acquired 200,000 pounds, "honestly gotten and unenvied, which
is next to a miracle",[18] according to Evelyn. The King had a warm
esteem for Sir Stephen. On 14th September 1681 Evelyn dined
with Fox, who

> propos'd to me ye purchasing of Chelsea Colledge, which his
> Ma^{tr} had some time since given to our Society, and would now
> purchase it againe to build an hospital or infirmary for souldiers
> there, in which he desired my assistance as one of the Council of
> the Royal Society.[19]

At the end of January 1682, Sir Stephen again informed Evelyn
of Charles II's resolution of proceeding in the building of a
Royal Hospital "for emerited souldiers on that spot of ground
which the Royal Society had sold to his Ma^{tr} for £1,300". On
4th August Evelyn accompanied Sir Stephen Fox "to survey the
foundation of the Royal Hospital at Chelsea". Dr. Richard
Eyre, preaching the sermon at Sir Stephen Fox's funeral, certainly
supports Evelyn's statement. He mentioned that "he was the first
projector of the noble design of Chelsea Hospital, and contributed
to the expence of it, above £13,000". (Fox's contribution was in
fact £1,300.) Dr. Eyre went on to say that Fox could not bear to
see "the common soldiers beg at our doors" and therefore did
what he could to remove such a scandal to the kingdom.

Charles II was certainly keenly interested in the project for the
Royal Hospital.[25] On 16th December 1681 Nicholas Johnson was
appointed treasurer for the hospital, while in early January 1682,
Sir Christopher Wren informed the Council of the Royal Society
that he had agreed, subject to the Council's approval, to sell
Chelsea College to Fox "for His Majesty's use". Charles II
contributed 6,787 pounds from the Secret Service Money, with
interest amounting to 1,174 pounds to build the hospital. It took
ten years to erect, and was at last completed during the reign of
King William III and Queen Mary in 1692.

There is a tradition that Nell Gwyn lived for a while at Sand-
ford Manor House in Chelsea, and her mother certainly died in

---

* 1627–1726. He was once a choirboy in Salisbury Cathedral.

some neat house in Chelsea during July 1679. A contemporary recorded: "Elen Gwynne commonly called Old Madam Gwynne, being drunk with brandy, fell in a ditch neare the neat houses London and was stifled."[21]

Nell was painted by Sir Peter Lely, who died in 1680; by Henri Gascar; by Simon Verelst, and other artists. The Army and Navy Club are proud of their fine Sir Peter Lely portrait in a brown satin dress, and this artist's paintings of her in the nude* are very attractive. The National Portrait Gallery possesses several Lelys, of Nell Gwyn. One of these aroused considerable controversy during the tercentenary year of her birth (1950), when it was alleged that the portrait was in reality that of Catherine Sedley, Countess of Dorchester, the mistress of James II. She was as witty as Nelly, but possessed neither her charm, agreeable personality, nor her extreme prettiness. Indeed, Catherine was an ugly, coarse woman. It may have been of her that Charles II remarked, "I believe that my brother has his mistresses given him by his priests for penance,"[22] A scurrilous writer referred to her:

> Lo, thy daughter, little Sid,†
> She who lately slipt her kid.
> Sure a hopeful Babe 'twill be,
> Soak'd in Pox and Popery.

Lord Thomas Bruce, who served Charles II as a gentleman of his bedchamber, idolized his master. He relates in his memoirs how the King would pull off his hat, when sauntering in the galleries and the park, to the meanest of his subjects. Writing in exile in Brussels many years later, Lord Bruce—now Earl of Ailesbury— nostalgically recalled the "unspeakable delight" of the King's company. Though Charles was extremely affable, he could sometimes put on majesty if the occasion warranted it. When Sir Thomas Vernon intruded into His Majesty's bedchamber, the King's face was so severe that Sir Thomas disappeared as fast as he had come. "And I never saw a poor gentleman so ashamed," added Ailesbury.

* Charles II liked to watch his mistress being painted by Lely.
† Sir Charles Sedley. The Lady Catherine Darnley, his granddaughter, was to become the third wife of John Sheffield Duke of Buckingham. The Duchess of Buckingham, in fact, became a keen Protestant.

During 1684 Charles at last had the satisfaction of knowing that he had triumphed over his enemies. Two years earlier Lord Shaftesbury had been forced to take refuge in Holland, where he died during 1682. During his last years, however, Charles was increasingly anxious as to what would happen to his brother James when he ascended the throne. Once, when he was walking in Hyde Park with Sir Richard Bulstrode, the King, in a melancholy mood, confided to Bulstrode: "I am weary of travelling, and am resolved to go abroad no more. But when I am dead and gone, I know not what my brother will do; I am much afraid that when he comes to wear the crown he will be obliged to travel again. And yet I will take care to leave my Kingdoms to him in peace, wishing he may long keep them so. But this hath all of my fears, little of my hopes and less of my reason."[23] With incanny prescience the King had glimpsed for a moment the dark, uncertain future.

During the summer of 1683 there arrived at the Court at Whitehall a young Frenchman aged 28, named Philippe de Vendôme* a nephew of the Duchesse Mazarin. Philippe de Vendôme was grandson of Henri IV, and of one of his mistresses, Gabrielle d'Estrées, known as "La Belle Gabrielle". This certainly endeared him to the Duchess of Portsmouth. It was evident to the English courtiers that the young French nobleman did everything to ingratiate himself with Her Grace of Portsmouth, for he had heard of the great wealth she had accumulated in England. Louise too, was known to be cold and calculating, could not disguise her tenderness for her compatriot. For long hours the two were closeted together in Louise's luxurious apartments, until Charles II's jealousy was aroused. There can be little doubt that Louise temporarily became Vendôme's mistress. She was 35 at this period and, if her portrait by Pierre Mignard in the National Portrait Gallery can be relied on, she had already lost much of her beauty. The fat, astute Paul Barillon, French Ambassador in London, uneasily aware of the amorous intrigue, kept Louis XIV fully informed about it. It was feared by Lord Sunderland that Louise's wanton behaviour would jeopardize her ascendancy at Court. Once the King's suspicions became proofs, Louise would no

* Grand Prior of France.

longer be able to maintain her dominating position. Her many enemies exulted that the hated favourite would at last be disgraced. Rumours, almost certainly invented by her enemies, had always plagued her. Earlier in 1679 it was reported that a Mr. Brandon Gerard "had been forbidden the Court for getting the French She (Portsmouth) with child and that a blackamore comes betwixt her quarters".[24]

The King was almost 54, and fast ageing. He certainly could not stomach this Frenchman playing the wanton with his mistress. So he determined that the Grand Prior must be banished the country. De Vendôme was loath to go, but at the end of September he set sail for Holland and eventually returned to France. Barillon was instructed by Louis XIV to let Her Grace of Portsmouth know that, if De Vendôme ever said anything derogatory about her, he would justly incur the resentment of the French King.[25]

It must be said that Louise was far too clever a woman not to behave with circumspection and tact. All the same, there are solid reasons for believing that the King was tiring of his French favourite during his last year. Thomas second Earl of Ailesbury, when in exile many years later, wrote of his recollection of his beloved master's last days.* "He had an habitual custom to go after meals to the Duchess of Portsmouth's for to amuse himself with the company that ate there . . ., and I have good reason to believe that he was seeking by degrees to have her to retire."[26] Perhaps Louise's sly intrigue with the French nobleman was a woman's subtle revenge for the humiliation she had suffered eight years before, when the King had neglected her for the Duchesse Mazarin.

* He was then Lord Thomas Bruce.

Death of Charles II

FOR the last time the lovely voice of Henry Bowman could be heard at one of Nell Gwyn's musical parties, giving voice to James Shirley's song, a special favourite of the King's.

> The glories of our blood and state
> Are shadows, not substantial things.
> There is no armour against fate;
> Death lays his icy hand on Kings.

It was late 1684, almost the end of an era. As she watched Charles's harsh face suddenly grow gentle under the influence of the music, did a foreboding come to Nelly that the words of this song would prove strangely prophetic? Her contemporaries thought she was giddy, but towards the end of her short life Nell was increasingly pensive and anxious about what would happen to her when the King died. True, the King had enjoyed superb health, but there were signs that he was growing tired. He now confined himself to a short walk twice daily in the garden of Arlington House or St. James's Park. During the late winter of '84 to '85 Charles had a running sore on one of his legs, and, instead of walking, was obliged to take the air in a calash, attended by the tall young Lord Thomas Bruce, who was rapidly becoming a favourite.

It was a cruel winter, and frosts were particularly severe, so that the Thames was sometimes frozen over. On Sunday 1st February 1685 Dr. Dove preached before the King. John Evelyn, who happened to be at Court that evening, wrote disapprovingly in his diary: "I saw this evening such a scene of profuse gaming, and the King in the midst of his three concubines, as I had never before seen. Luxurious dallying and prophaneness."[1] Nell was not included among the three concubines, since she was not present on that evening. Two at least of the three concubines mentioned by

Evelyn, Barbara Villiers Duchess of Cleveland and Hortense Mancini Duchesse of Mazarin, were no longer mistresses, while the Duchess of Portsmouth was now more a favourite companion than a mistress. The Duchess of Cleveland still retained a trace of her former loveliness, while the Duchesse Mazarin's face "was beautiful with the rich beauty of the South".[2] While the King dallied with his three sultanas, Hortense's French page, a handsome boy with an exquisite voice, warbled love songs in that splendid gallery. About twenty of the dissolute courtiers were engrossed in a game of basset round a large table whence came the chink of gold.

The evening was full of memories for Charles II, and when Lord Thomas Bruce, as was his duty, came to light the King to his bedchamber door, he handed the large wax candle to the page of the back stairs. Though there was no wind, the candle suddenly went out. The page significantly shook his head, for he happened to be superstitious. Long afterwards writing in exile, Lord Bruce, now second Earl of Ailesbury, remembered how particularly charming the King was on that evening. He talked longingly about his house, which was in process of being built near Winchester. He remarked to Bruce that he could not remember ever having seen him there. When Bruce modestly replied that he never liked to intrude himself, the King replied: "Odsfish! Modesty must sooner or later be rewarded and when 'tis otherwise, 'tis the fault of the sovereign and not of the subject."

It was an uneasy night in the royal bedchamber. There was constant noise from the chiming of the clocks, and a dozen dogs of the King's roamed about the room. As it was very cold, a great fire sizzled with Scotch coal. Bruce noticed that his master stirred restlessly in his sleep, although he was used to all this noise.

Next morning, just as the King's barber was about to shave him, the King had a fit of apoplexy, and fell into the arms of the faithful Lord Bruce. It was fortunate that Bruce was present, for he at once ordered the royal physician, Doctor King, who was standing by, to bleed His Majesty. While Bruce hastily left to fetch the Duke of York, the King was laid in his bed. When Charles saw Bruce again at his bedside, he had recovered his conciousness, and said, "I see you love me dying as well as living."

Lord Macaulay in his brilliant account of the last scenes of Charles's life, relates that "during a short time, the Duchess of Portsmouth hung over him with the familiarity of a wife".[3] No contemporary account, however, mentions this, except Bishop Burnet's statement, who was prejudiced. Louise herself told Barillon, the French Ambassador, "I cannot with decency enter the room, besides that the Queen is almost constantly there."[4] We know that Queen Catherine of Braganza knelt for long hours at his bedside, and that he spoke tender words to her. When no longer able to endure the hours of waiting, the Queen sent a message, asking her husband to excuse her, and begged his pardon if she had offended him. Charles then murmured, "Alas, poor woman! She beg my pardon! I beg hers with all my heart." When told by his doctors not to talk, Charles remarked with a flash of his old wit that such an order would be the death of his friend Harry Killigrew.

It is strange to relate that Charles's fatal last illness occurred on 2nd February, which was Nell Gwyn's thirty-fifth birthday.[5] It is easy to imagine Nell's feelings during the next few days, for she truly loved him. It was agonizing for her to hear about his sufferings and not to be present in the royal bedchamber. None of Charles's mistresses would have been allowed access there, for it would have been deemed indecent. From others she was forced to hear about the constant purgings and bleedings ordered by his doctors, and how the Protestant clergyman, led by the gentle Archbishop Sancroft and the fiery Bishop Ken of Bath and Wells, incessantly exhorted the King to receive the Anglican sacraments. It was the same Thomas Ken, who had once denied her a lodging at Winchester.

She would have also heard that Charles, a secret Catholic for many years, had shown a desire during his last hours to be received into the arms of the Catholic Church. Was it Queen Catherine of Braganza, who had sensed his need, or the Duchess of Portsmouth, closeted alone with Paul Barillon, the French Ambassador, in her luxurious apartments, now deserted, in the palace? Was it the cherished memory of that beloved sister Minette, who had so longed for him to join the Catholic Church, persuading him at the end? It is true that Louise told Barillon in the privacy of her apartments, that she was certain the King at the bottom of his heart was a Catholic. "*Monsieur l'Ambassadeur,*" she assured him, "it is a great secret, and I would lose my head, if it were known."[6] If the King were to be saved, he must immediately see a priest. Barillon hurried back into the royal bedchamber, and made some excuses to take the Duke of York aside. The Duke then whispered in his brother's ear, "Do you desire to see a priest, Sire?" The King was heard to say with difficulty, "Yes, with all my heart!" A priest named Father John Huddleston,* who had saved Charles's life after the battle of Worcester, was then smuggled, disguised, up the back stairs into the royal bedchamber by the resourceful Chiffinch. There the anguished King received the final rites of the Catholic Church. Nell Gwyn, who had known Charles so well, had also been aware that he was a secret Catholic. There are indications that after his death she wished to share that communion.

On the last evening of his life the King gave his blessing to his natural sons, who were brought to his bedside. These were the Duke of St. Albans, the Duke of Richmond, and the Dukes of Grafton, Southampton, and Northumberland, sons of the Duchess of Cleveland. According to Macaulay, Charles spoke with peculiar tenderness to Richmond. The King never once mentioned the Duke of Monmouth, who was in exile in Holland.

That night Charles remembered Nelly with some of the best known words in history. He conjured his brother James, who had been constantly at his bedside, "Do not let poor Nelly starve."[7] John Evelyn related: "He spoke to the Duke to be kind to the Dutchesse of Cleaveland, and especially Portsmouth, and that Nelly might not starve."

February 6th dawned, a pale spectral day, and, as the morning light began to filter into the darkened room, Charles II asked his servants to draw back the curtains, so that he might see the daylight for the last time. He reminded his attendants that they should wind up a clock, which stood near his bed. With exquisite courtesy and wit he apologized to those who had attended him all night, for the trouble he had caused and that he had been "an unconsciable time a-dying". Nell Gwyn, no doubt overcome with

* Charles II had preserved his life during the Popish terror.

grief, first became aware of the King's death when she heard the tolling of the bells. No King has been more sincerely mourned than Charles II, and the groans of his subjects could be heard in the streets.

It is almost certain that Nell Gwyn for some time was attracted by the notion that she might possibly join the Roman Catholics as a convert, thus sharing in the communion of her beloved King. Artistic, impulsive people like her are often attracted to the sensual loveliness and ritual of the Roman Catholic religion. They say their prayers at the Brompton Oratory, without really intending to join that Church. Evelyn, in his derisory way, mentions that Mrs. Nelly accompanied by her old friend John Dryden and his two sons were said to go to mass. "Such proselytes," he added, "were no greate losse to the Church."* Since Dryden had satirized Roman Catholic priests in his play, *The Spanish Friar*, and had formerly seemed hostile to that Church, it is possible that he now wished to curry favour with James II when he attended mass. Whatever his motives were, he became a Catholic. During the last years, Nell Gwyn came under the influence of Dr. Richard Lower, a fervent Protestant, and Dr. Thomas Tenison,† vicar of St. Martin-in-the-fields and later Archbishop of Canterbury. She always adhered to the Protestant religion.

During 1685 it is evident that Nell was in acute financial difficulties. After Charles's death, some of her creditors came to 79 Pall Mall, swooping on her like a flock of vultures and demanding their debts should be paid. Though not actually arrested for debt, she was outlawed for the non-payment of various bills. At this critical juncture, Nell was compelled to appeal to the benevolence of James II. To his lasting honour, the new king was faithful to his brother's dying request: "Do not let poor Nelly starve."

There are in the British Museum two undated letters,[8] dictated by Nell to a secretary and sent to the new king. In the first letter it is clear that she is seeking an interview with James. She wrote:

Had I suferd for my God as I have don for yr brother and you, I should not have needed other of yr kindnes or justice to me. I beseech you not to doe anything to the setling of my buisnes till I

---

* 19th January 1686.   † 1636–1715.

speake with you and apoynt me by Mr. Grahams when I may
speake with you privetly. God make you as happy as my soule
prayes you may be,

y^{rs}.

This letter is unsigned. Perhaps Nell was familiar with Wolsey's
speech in *Henry the Eighth*, when the mighty Cardinal has fallen
from power. So too was she deprived of her influence at Court.

Her second letter to the King is more hopeful and jubilant.

S^r, [she dictated]
This world is not capable of giving me a greater joy and happynes
than y^r Maties favour, not as you are King and, soe have it in y^r
poer, to doe me good, having never loved y^r brother and y^r selfe
upon that account, but as to y^r persons. Had hee lived, hee tould
me before hee dyed, that the world shuld see by what hee did for
me that hee had both love and value for me, and that hee did not
doe for me as my mad Lady Woster.* He was my friend and
allowed me to tell him all my grifes, and did like a frind advise me
and tould me who was my frind and who was not.[9]

If he had lived, Charles II had intended to create Nell Gwyn
Countess of Greenwich. It is clear that Nell had troubles of her
own, and was in the habit of confiding in Charles II concerning
them. It is touching to imagine the King in the rôle of a comforter
to one of his favourite mistresses.

If we consult the accounts of the Secret Service in the reign of
James II, we realize that Richard Graham, during 1685, on behalf
of the King, paid Mrs. Ellen Gwyn's debts to various tradesmen
and creditors. These debts amounted to £729 2s 3d.[10] In such a
way did James II in his conscientious way relieve her of her most
pressing debts. In the course of the same year two sums of 500
pounds each were paid to her as bounty. Towards the end of 1686,
Nell Gwyn was by no means free from financial difficulties. Among
the archives of Messrs. Glyn, Mills, the Bankers, there is a note
from James Booth to Mr. Child her banker. "Mr. Child. Madame
Gwyne desires you will send her the balance of the account which
I had from Mr. Jackson of Seventy-three pounds. This note my
Lady commanded me to send you last night.—I am, sir, your

* Margaret Somerset, Marchioness of Worcester.

humble servant James Booth,"—Pall Mall, 10th December, 1686.

It was a bitter blow for Nell to have to part with one of her most treasured possessions, the lovely pearl necklace she had bought from Peg Hughes.

Her Last Years

WHEN Sir John Germain, a coarse courtier of Dutch
extraction tried to persuade Nell Gwyn in 1686 to sleep
with him, she would have none of him. Nell told Mary,
Duchess of Norfolk, in her characteristic way "that she would not
lay the dog where the deer laid, for she knew my lady duchess
would accept of him."[1] Indeed over four years after Nell's death,
the Duke of Norfolk was obliged to commence proceedings in the
House of Lords for his marriage to be dissolved on account of his
wife's adultery with Germaine. The State trial is a fascinating
study.

One of the witnesses, named Mrs. Benskin, a servant of the
Duke and Duchess of Norfolk, gave evidence that on one occasion
her mistress and Germaine had travelled together from Windsor.
On returning to her house, the Duchess had ordered a fire to be
lit in her husband's room. Mrs. Nelly Gwyn then came in and
remarked to the Duchess, "Good morrow to your Grace; how
did you rest last night?" When she asked after Germaine, the
Duchess said she knew nothing of him. My Lady complaining of
her hair being out of order, Nell answered, "It was a hot night
with her, enough to put her hair out of powder and curl too."[2]
It was the kind of impudent remark one would expect from
Nelly. When another visitor, a Colonel Cornwall, inquired about
Germaine, the Duchess of Norfolk denied all knowledge of him.
Mrs. Nelly then delightfully said, "We will see him come out
bye-and-bye like a drowned rat." The trial in Westminster Hall
caused a great sensation. It was not, however, until 1700 that the
Duke of Norfolk succeeded in obtaining an Act of Parliament for
a divorce.

Nell was deeply saddened in April 1687 by the death of her old

friend, the Duke of Buckingham, known more familiarly to his
friends as the 'Duke of Bucks'. He had been in poor health for
some time, and during 1686 had been living on his estate at
Helmesley in Yorkshire, where he passed the time hunting and
drinking heavily with his cronies. After a fox hunt, Buckingham
was unwise enough to catch a chill from sitting on the damp
ground. He was carried to a tenant's lonely farmhouse at Kirkby-
Moorside, where he was given the best bedroom.[3]

The account of his death in the Ellis Correspondence is in-
correct. It relates:

> The Duke of Bucks, who hath some time supported himself with
> artificial spirits, on Friday fell to a more manifest decay, and on
> Sunday yielded up the ghost at Helmesley, in Yorkshire, in a little
> ale house (where these eight months he hath been without meat
> or money, deserted of all his servants, almost).

He was given a magnificent funeral in Westminster Abbey.

Sir Charles Sedley, whom Nell had known well in her early life,
lived on until 1701, He later became a warm partisan of King
William III, remarking, as he came out of the House of Commons,
when William and Mary were proclaimed King and Queen in
1689: "Well, I am even with King James, in point of civility. For
as he made my daughter a Countess (Dorchester), so I have helped
to make his daughter a Queen."

During 1687 Nell was very seriously ill. The Ellis Correspondence records: "Mrs Nelly is dying of an apoplexy, her son (the
Duke of St. Albans) will go for Hungary, and return a good
Catholic, as thought." Clifford Bax,* however, who studied the
medical evidence, thinks that she was suffering from 'the pox',
transmitted to her by Charles II. During her illness in March
1687 part of her body was completely paralysed. Although James
II attempted to proselytize the young Duke of St. Albans, who
was now 17, he adhered to the Protestant religion. Catherine of
Braganza, now Queen-Dowager, had always liked Nell Gwyn's
son and now generously agreed to grant him an allowance of
2,000 a year.

Charles Duke of St. Albans possessed no great ability. He

* *Pretty Witty Nelly.*

certainly inherited his father's and his mother's courage, for he
served in the Emperor's Army at the Siege of Belgrade and
acquitted himself valiantly when the Austrians wrested it from the
Turks during 1688. If Nell Gwyn had survived the year 1687, it
is almost certain that her sympathies would have been for the
Jacobites. A few of her friends, however, like Henry Sidney, were
Whigs. Would she have disapproved when her son, on taking his
seat in the House of Lords, joined the Whigs? We cannot be
certain.

During his father's lifetime, the Duke of St. Albans had been
betrothed to an heiress, the Earl of Oxford's daughter, Lady
Diana de Vere, who was a beauty, but the marriage did not take
place until 1694, after Nell Gwyn's death. They had a large family
of twelve children. William III seems to have favoured him, for
he created him Captain of the band of Gentlemen Pensioners and
a Lord of the Bedchamber. He held many prominent posts, including the offices of High Steward of Windsor and Wokingham.
During the reign of George I he was installed a Knight of the
Garter at Windsor. He died at Bath in 1726.

Many will be curious to know what happened to Nell's rival in
the affections of Charles II, the avaricious Duchess of Portsmouth.
She returned to France, a very wealthy woman, her English
estate worth 5,000 pounds a year. She had invested huge sums in
France and possessed jewels of great value. Voltaire, who knew
her in later life, relates that she was still a handsome women. He
described her at 70 "*avec une figure encore noble et agréable, que les
années n'avaient point flétrie,*"* She survived Charles II by almost
half a century, dying on 14th November 1734, aged 85. It is
perhaps a coincidence that she died on the same day and during
the same month as Nell Gwyn, but forty-seven years later.

Very different, was the fate of the lovely Hortense Mancini
Duchesse Mazarin. During the early summer of 1699, Hortense,
who was living in the village of Chelsea, fell seriously ill. She
died on 2nd July, gravely embarrassed by debts and mourned
by her devoted friend Charles Marguetel de St. Denis, Seigneur
de St. Evremonde.

In October 1709—twenty-two years after Nell—there died at

* With a face still noble and pleasing, that the years had never withered.

L

her home in Chiswick Mall, Barbara Villiers Duchess of Cleveland. Four years earlier, after her husband's death, she had married an adventurer named Beau Fielding, who had treated her abominably, although no pity should be wasted on her. How often had Nell referred to Barbara's brats by the King, though she had once given the sailor Duke of Grafton a generous present.

What is the final verdict on the character of Nell Gwyn? Colley Cibber, who had the advantage of talking to those who had known her during her lifetime, wrote charitably enough:

> But if we consider her in all the disadvantages of her rank and education, she does not appear to have had any criminal errors more remarkable than her sex's frailty to answer for; . . . Yet if the common fame of her may be believ'd, which in my memory was not doubted, she had less to be laid to her charge than any other of those Ladies, who were in the same state of preferment; she never meddled in matters of serious moment, or was the tool of working politicians: Never broke into those amourous infidelities which others in that grave author [Bishop Burnet] are accus'd of; but was as visibly distinguish'd by her particular personal inclination to the King, as her rivals were by their titles and grandeur.[4]

It is true that her love for the King was to some extent disinterested. Burnet, however, rightly maintained that Mrs. Gwyn acted all persons in so lively a manner and was of such a constant diversion to the King that even a new mistress could not drive her away. She was indeed the most endearing of Charles II's loves.

This indeed remains a just estimate of Nell Gwyn's character. Although she might appear giddy to her intimates, and was sometimes deceived by so-called intriguing friends, she had plenty of common sense. The secret of her hold over Charles II for sixteen years was that he could relax with her. She was never hysterical, like Lady Castlemaine, or prone to tears, like Louise de Kéroualle. She was immoral, and never pretended to be otherwise. Yet we can excuse her for her frailty of nature, considering her appalling upbringing. Although she was sensual and pleasure-loving, she had some refinement of spirit, for she enjoyed the society of John Dryden and Sir Robert Howard. She almost certainly possessed more feeling for literature than has been imagined. While she remained Charles's mistress, she was always loyal to him, and it would seem that she was faithful to his memory after his death She was never a sentimentalist, for the raw life of the London streets in her childhood remained a vivid experience. Compassionate by nature, she not only pitied the lot of those less fortunate than herself but was generous, too. In her will she remembered the poor debtors of the parish of St. Martin-in-the-Fields, and requested that a hundred pounds should be bequeathed them, to get them out of prison and to buy them warm clothing for the winter. Of all the remarkable personalities, who "strutted and fretted their hour upon the stage" during the Restoration Age, it is Nell Gwyn who is most cherished, even more than Charles II, or Samuel Pepys, who had so admired her. Although her ambition to be ennobled was frustrated, she had the satisfaction of founding a ducal house.

There was formerly an ancient custom at the Savoy Chapel, which has now fallen into abeyance. On the Sunday following Christmas Day it was usual to place near the door of the chapel a chair covered with a cloth, on which was placed an orange in a plate. When Nell became a favourite of Charles II, it is almost certain that she would occasionally attend the Savoy Chapel. Is it too fanciful to suppose that this custom commemorates Nell, who was once an orange-wench, a recognized profession in Restoration Days?

In her lucid moments when she was ill during the last year of her life did Nell ever return in spirit to the scene of her great triumphs, 'The King's House?' In that twilight world between sleeping and waking, was she ever pursued by dreams of long ago? Now she is back in the theatre, and the excited faces of her audience glow in the soft candle-light, shadowy and aetherial like pale ghosts. She is playing Florimel, and an enchanting smile transfigures her face as she relishes once again the sauciness of the part. She had owed so much to Charles Hart, who is Celadon in *Secret Love*. She could almost hear his rich sonorous voice. He had told her, "An actor must always forget himself in the rôle he is portraying."

Florimel: But this marriage is such a Bugbear to me; much might be if we could invent by any way to make it easie.

Celadon: Some foolish people have made it uneasie, by drawing
     the knot faster than they need; but we that are wiser will
     loosen it a little.

Now she dons men's habit and addresses herself: "Faith methinks
you are a very jaunty fellow, poudré and adjusté as well as the
best of 'em." Now she is Valerie speaking the epilogue in
Tyrannick Love, and the audience has hardly recovered from their
surprise that she is still their Nelly alive. How dare the bearers
take her away!

     For after Death, we sprights have just such natures,
     We had for all the world, when humane creatures.

How the audience had responded when she confided to them that
she would "play all my tricks in Hell, a goblin there". What a
wonderful life she had experienced! From orange-wench, to leading actress, and then mistress to "her Charles the Third".

Now she was 37 and felt that death might be imminent. She
frankly admitted that she had been a sinner in some respects, no
worse than many others. During the last months of her life, Nell
Gwyn derived much comfort from the visits of Dr. Thomas
Tenison, vicar of St. Martin-in-the-Fields, to her Pall Mall house.
Dr. Tenison was now 51, and was recognized in his own age as an
extremely fine preacher. He had first come into prominence in
1680. Evelyn had a high opinion of him, and found "his holy conversation, very learned and ingenuous". "The pains he takes and
care of his parish will, I feare, weare him out, which would be an
inexpressible loss,"[5] Evelyn need not have been afraid, for Thomas
Tenison survived until 1715. It is probable that Nell had first become acquainted with Tenison through Dr. Richard Lower,* an
uncompromising Protestant, who attended her during her various
illnesses.

Dr. Lower was an extremely talented physiologist, who had
been born at Tremeer near Bodmin in Cornwall. Richard Lower
was a zealous Protestant and, like many Cornishmen, deeply
interested in politics. He was a member of the Whig party.
Anthony à Wood, quoting Bishop Kennet, wrote about him: "I
have heard Dr. Tenison, Archbishop of Canterbury, say often of

* 1631-1691.

him that Dr. Lower was his special friend, and had the Protestant interest much at heart. . . ." Lower got on splendidly with Nell Gwyn. After all they were both Celts. He often visited her, "and would pick out of her all the intrigues of the Court of Charles II". He was strongly opposed to the policy of James II, and that sovereign would say of him "that he did him more mischief than a troop of horse". Richard Lower had been frequently consulted during Charles II's last illness, and no doctor except for Dr. Charles Scarburgh had been so constantly in attendance.[6]

It is evident that Tenison found Nell penitent, and always possessed kindly feelings for her. Nell no doubt liked to talk with the vicar of St. Martin-in-the-Fields about the Duke of Monmouth, for Tenison had attended him before his execution in 1685. Sadly, she would have recalled her past friendship with 'Prince Perkin', Charles II's misguided son.

On 9th July 1687, Nell made her will,* appointing as her executors her friends Laurence Hyde Earl of Rochester, the Hon. Henry Sidney, Thomas Earl of Pembroke, and Sir Robert Sawyer, the Attorney-General. She signed only 'E.G.' The Earl of Pembroke† was very learned, especially in mathematics, and two years later became President of the Royal Society (1689–90). Sir Robert Sawyer, "a dull, fat man" in Bishop Burnet's opinion, "and forward to serve all the designs of the Court", had prosecuted the ringleaders after the Rye House Plot. The five witnesses to Nell's will were Lucy Hamilton Sandy's, Edward Wybourne, John Warner, William Scarborough and James Booth. Lucy Hamilton Sandys was the Lady Sandys for whom Nell had hired a sedan-chair to take her to the theatre. James Booth had often acted as her secretary. She left her estate to "my dear natural son, His Grace the Duke of St. Albans and the heirs of his body". Nell provided that "my said executers shall have all and every one of them one hundred pounds a piece of lawfull money, in consideration of their care and trouble herein, and furthermore, all there several and respective expenses" regarding her will.

Nell's codicil to her will added a month before her death,

* I have studied a copy in Somerset House, but Cunningham printed it in his book.
† 1656–1733.

provides further evidence, if it were needed, of her charitable and
kindly nature. It was called 'the last request of Mrs. Ellen Gwynn
to His Grace the Duke of St. Albans, made October 18th 1687."
It provided:

(1) I desire that I may be buried in the Church of St. Martin-in-
the-Fields.
(2) That Dr. Tenison may preach my funeral sermon.
(3) That there may be a decent pulpit-cloth and cushion given to
St. Martin-in-the-Fields.
(4) That he (the Duke of St. Albans) would give one hundred
pounds for the use of the poor of the said St. Martin's and
St. James's Westminster, to be given into the hands of the said
Dr. Tenison . . . for taking any poor debtors of the said parish
out of prison, and for cloaths this winter, and other necessaries
as he shall find most fit.
(5) That for showing my charity to those who differ from me in
religion, I desire that £50 may be put into the hands of Dr.
Tenison and Mr. Warner, who taking to them any two persons
of the Roman religion, may dispose of it for the use of the poor
of that religion inhabiting the parish of St. James's aforesaid.
(This clearly reveals that Nell lacked all bigotry.)
(6) That Mrs. Rose Forster (her sister) may have two hundred
pounds given to her, any time within a year after my decease.
(7) That Jo, my porter, may have Ten pounds given to him.
(8) My request to His Grace is further that my present nurses may
have ten pounds and mourning, besides their wages due to each.

Lastly Nell requested her son to lay out twenty pounds yearly for
the releasing of poor debtors out of prison, every Christmas Day.
It was Dr. Christianus Harrell, and not Dr. Richard Lower, who
attended her in her last illness. She left him twenty pounds.
Harrell had also been present at Charles II's deathbed. This distinguished doctor, born at the Hague, was of German-Dutch
extraction, and he became a Fellow of the Royal College of
Physicians. It is related that he wrote English like a foreigner and
French correctly. Among the interesting documents in the archives
of Messrs. Glyn, Mills the Bankers, is a receipt signed by Christianus Harrell (he spelled it Harel), showing that he was given
109 pounds, which "paid in full of all remedies and medicins

delivred to Mrs. Ellin Gwyn deceased". This sum was paid by Mr. Child, Nell's banker, only three days after her death. Harrell must have wished that Charles II's account had been settled as promptly, but the King was included among his *'Listes des Debtes Desperates'*. It amounted to 1,527 pounds 10 shillings. He subsequently became physician in ordinary to King William III and Queen Mary II.

Gradually during that autumn Nell Gwyn's health had been getting weaker. She died on 14th November 1687, at her house, 79 Pall Mall. Narcissus Luttrell records: "Mrs. Ellen Gwyn was buried the 17th November at St. Martins; she hath left a considerable estate to her son, the Duke of St. Albans."[7]

St. Martin-in-the-Fields was crowded with her admirers when Dr. Thomas Tenison preached his funeral sermon on 17th November. It is a misfortune that it has not survived. He would have spoken with eloquence and infinite understanding about her and referred to her sincere penitence. Later, during the reign of King William and Queen Mary, a critic of Tenison's tried to prevent his promotion to the bishopric of Lincoln because he had been courageous enough, despite the disapproval of some people, to preach her funeral sermon—a heinous sin in their eyes. Queen Mary, however, supported the claims of the distinguished cleric, declaring very sensibly and with unusual charity, "If I can read a man's heart through his looks, had she not made a truly pious end the Doctor could never have been induced to speak well of her."

Nell Gwyn would certainly have been distressed, if Dr. Tenison's promotion to a bishopric had been postponed because of her.

It was fortunate for her that she lived during the Restoration era and not today. In the age of candlelight her genius could flourish for a while on the stage, to delight and astonish her contemporaries. There never existed any danger that her irresistible spirits would be crushed or smothered by the taboos of our own time. Ultimately she triumphed over her rivals. She is loved and cherished, and her name still inspires and evokes tender memories.

APPENDIX

Nell Gwyn's Horoscope

by

JOHN NAYLOR
President, Federation of British Astrologers

What constitutes the horoscope of a female 'charmer' or courtesan? A surprising number of much-married, twentieth-century 'sex symbols' were born under the sign Libra. Brigitte Bardot and Rita Hayworth are two who immediately spring to mind.

Women born under the 'air' signs, Gemini, Libra, Aquarius, tend to have strong sex-appeal without being strongly sexed physically. Their approach to love and sex is idealistic and fastidious. They need soft lights, sweet music, much verbal and physical caressing before they are emotionally and sexually aroused. To stimulate the male to meet their needs they cultivate the arts of flirtation!

Aquarius subjects, both male and female, are predisposed towards unorthodox, unconventional relationships. They incline towards marriage in which there is a disparity of age or background, racially mixed marriages, and to dispense with the orthodox church blessing. Aquarian women are seldom happily domesticated. They have a need of independent interests and activities outside the home.

Nell Gwyn was an Aquarius subject. She was born just after a new moon and her horoscope shows the Sun in Aquarius, the Moon in the last degree of Aquarius in conjunction with Mars. The Sun, Mercury, Mars and the Moon are all in Aquarius. The sign Capricorn and the planet Venus are on the Ascendant of the horoscope.

These factors suggest that Nell was a tantalizing witch, provocative, unpredictable, surprisingly independent in thought and action—a very distinct 'personality'.

Her off-beat angle on people and events, her complete lack of conventional inhibitions, were qualities which helped her to ensnare Charles II. Her fatal fascination was her prettiness and wit—not her performance in bed! Charles II is remembered as a playboy. He was also founder of the Royal Society. Nell's quick and inventive intellect appealed to him.

Due to the Capricorn Ascendant to her horoscope, Nell was a practical idealist. Combined with the characteristics already mentioned was a strata of tough, shrewd practicality. This does not mean that she was a gold-digger. It means that she was a basically creative, ingenious person, who tried to give her talents practical application. If born in the twentieth century she would have provided keen competition for Mary Quant (the pioneer of a 'new look' in women's fashions) or actress/social reformer Vanessa Redgrave. Both are fellow Aquarians, with horoscopes falling into the same category as Nell's.

In considering Nell Gwyn, remember that Aquarius produces brilliant inventors, artists, comedians; people who think in a fifth dimension, sensing aspects of life, thought, behaviour others are unaware of and conveying their unusual impressions in a brilliantly stimulating way.

As Nell's horoscope shows the Sun and Moon favourably aspected to Saturn, hers was quite a well-balanced and adjusted personality in maturity. There are no indications of acute psychological stresses due to family or childhood circumstances. The prominence of the two planets Venus and Neptune imply that Nell possessed artistic perception, that she was a music-lover. Incidentally, the strong Neptune suggests that she used a pseudonym during at least one period in her life.

A well-aspected Moon points to a potential for success through activities dependent on the response of the general public. The conjunction of the Moon with Mars indicates physical vitality and stamina. Nell's powers of moral and physical endurance were considerable.

To sum up. Nell was at core both a bohemian and an artist. She was a curious mixture of realist and visionary idealist. She was an individualist, possessing initiative and enterprise and therefore both physically and spiritually 'tough', yet had a responsive, sympathetic temperament.

In modern times she would have expressed her personality and talents in a successful career as a creative worker; her eventful and turbulent love life would have been a secondary consideration. As an entertainer she undoubtedly possessed a latent 'star quality'.

In the social conditions of the seventeenth century Nell expressed and developed her considerable talents in the role of mistress to royalty. 'Pretty, witty Nelly' was a woman of talent and character, probably providing in the seventeenth-century corridors of power the revolutionary, progressive inspiration now achieved at infinitely more effort and cost by the parliamentary opposition and various pressure groups. This quite apart from bringing happiness and pleasure to a royal lover!

According to ancient astrological lore people born four months apart, as were Nell and Charles II, are in affinity and make good partners!

NOTE

A contemporary horoscope for Nell Gwyn shows Capricorn 24° on the ascendant. My calculations produce an earlier degree of Capricorn. This is probably because the seventeenth-century astrologer, using a rough rule of thumb, arrived at the ascendant by calculating from the dawn position of the sun and allowing one degree for every four minutes of the difference between dawn and the time of birth. Uranus and Neptune, then unknown, are not shown on the seventeenth-century chart. A seventeenth-century ephemeris (or set of planetary times tables) was used when calculating the horoscopes, so that there are almost certainly errors, seventeenth-century astronomical techniques being less accurate than modern ones.

NOTES

CHAPTER I

1 *King Charles II*, p. 93.

2 *The Diary of Samuel Pepys*, with a life and Notes by Richard Lord Braybrook, 1660–1669.

3 Count Magalotti's account of the Travels of Cosmo the third Duke of Tuscany, through England during the reign of Charles II (1669).

4 Ibid.

5 *The Diary and Correspondence of Samuel Pepys*, 30th January 1665.

6 Ibid., 21st December 1663.

7 Correspondence of the Family of Hatton, being Chiefly Letters addressed to Christopher, 1st Viscount Hatton, A.D. 1601–1704.

8 Sir Charles Sedley, *Some Drinking Songs*, Brit. Mus. Add. MSS. 30, 382.

9 *The Rochester-Savile Letters, 1671–1681*, Edited by John Harold Wilson.

10 Count Magalotti's Account of the Travels of Cosmo the Third Duke of Tuscany.

CHAPTER II

1 Shelfmark MS. Ash. 423. Fol. 103, Bodleian Library.

2 John Wilmot Earl of Rochester, *Collected Works*, Nonesuch Press, 1926, p. 96.

3 Add. MSS. Brit. Mus., 26683, folio 59B.

4 Harleian MSS., Brit. Mus., 7319, folio 269.

5 *The Life and Times of Anthony à Wood, Antiquary of Oxford 1632–1695, described by himself.* Collected from his diaries and other papers, by Andrew Clark, M.A. Vol. II, 1684.

6 Volume LXXXVI C.S.P.D., Charles II.

7 Volume III, p. 278.

8 Macaulay, *History of England*, Vol. I, p. 161.

9 Colley Cibber, *Apology for his Life*, 2nd edition 8° 1740, Vol. 2.

10 Hotson, *Commonwealth and Restoration Stage*.

11 *Memoirs of John Evelyn*, comprising his diary from 1641–1705, Edited from the original MSS. by William Bray. Vol. 2, p. 140.

12 *Memoirs of Sir Richard Bulstrode.*

13 *Some Account of the English Stage from the Restoration in 1660–1830.* In 10 volumes by Rev. Genest, Vol. I.

14 W. J. MacQueen Pope, *Theatre Royal, Drury Lane.*

15 J. H. Wilson, *The Court Wits of the Restoration.* Princetown, 1948.

CHAPTER III

1 *The Story of Nell Gwynn and the Sayings of Charles the Second.* Related and Collected by Peter Cunningham.

2 Anthony Hamilton, *Memoirs of Count De Grammont*, p. 152.

3 Colley Cibber's *Apology for his Life*, 2nd edition 8°, 1740, Vol. 2.

4 Harleian MSS. 7319. 269.

5 Gerard Langbaine, *An Account of the English Dramatick Poets*, p. 317.

6 Dryden, *The Dramatic Works.* Nonesuch Press, Vol. I.

7 *The Diary of Samuel Pepys*, 21st June 1665.

8 *Calendar of State Papers Domestic*, Charles II, Vol. CXXXIX.

9 Sir Arthur Bryant, *King Charles II.*

10 *The Diary of Samuel Pepys*, Braybrooke Edn., Vol. 2. 19th March 1666.

11 *Calendar of State Papers*, Charles II, Vol. CLXVII.

CHAPTER IV

1 Page 6 as printed in an original edition of *The English Monsieur*, a comedy as it is acted at the Theatre Royal by His Majesty's Servants by the Hon. James Howard. Printed by H. Bruges for J. Magnus near the Piazza in Russel Street, Covent Garden (1674).

2 *Dramatic Miscellanies consisting of Critical Observations on several Plays of Shakespeare with a Review of His Principal Characters, and those of Various eminent Writers*, Thomas Davies, Vol. III.

3 Dryden, *The Dramatic Works.* Nonesuch Press, Vol. II.

4 *Dryden to Johnson*, edited by Boris Ford.

5 W. Carew Hazlitt, *A Select Collection of Old English Plays.* Originally published by Robert Dodsley in the year 1744.

6 V. De Solo Pinto, *Sir Charles Sedley 1639–1701. A Study in the Life and Literature of the Restoration* (1927).

7 From an interpolated Song in Etherege's *Man of Mode, or Sir Fopling Flutter*. Sung by Sir Carr Scrope or Sir Charles Sedley.

CHAPTER V

1 Charlotte Fell-Smith, *Mary Rich, Countess of Warwick, 1625–78*. Also see V. de Sola Pinto, *Sir Charles Sedley 1639–1701*.

2 Harleian MSS. 7319. 739. Brit. Mus.

3 Add. MSS. A.301 f. 194. Bodleian Library.

4 This document is among the Knole MSS. Ref. 075. A copy of a Signed Manual warrant to Lord Dorset, Sir Edward Villiers, and William Chiffinch Trustees of our "Trusty and well beloved Ellen Gwynn, holding Burford House in Trust, to make a best declaration of the Trust." (1683.)

CHAPTER VI

1 V. de Sola Pinto, *Sir Charles Sedley, 1639–1701. A Study in The Life and Literature of the Restoration.* (1927.)

2 Dryden, *The Dramatic Works*. The Nonesuch Press, Vol. II.

3 *Memoirs of John Evelyn, Esq., F.R.S., comprising His Diary from 1641 to 1705/6*. Vol. II. 19th June 1668.

4 Hesketh Pearson, *Charles II. His Life and Likeness*, p. 184 (1960).

5 *Some Account of the English Stage from the Restoration in 1660–1830.* Vol. I.

6 Colley Cibber, *Apology for his Life*, with notes and supplement. Edited by R. W. Lowe.

7 Hotson, *The Commonwealth and Restoration Stage*.

CHAPTER VII

1 *The History of My Own Time*. Clarendon Press, Vol. I, p. 474.

2 *History of the Court of England.*

3 *A Character of Charles II.*

4 *Transactions in England for the last hundred Years preceding the Revolution* (1688).

5 *England in the Reign of Charles II* (1934).

6 *The Life and Times of Anthony à Wood, Antiquary of Oxford, 1632–1695, described by himself.* Collected from his Diaries and other Papers.

7 Dryden, *The Dramatic Works*. Nonesuch Press, Vol. III.

8 *Apology for his Life*, with notes and supplement.

9 Dryden, *The Dramatic Works*. Nonesuch Press, Vol. III.

10 *Memoirs of John Evelyn*, Edited from the Original MSS. by William Bray. Vol. II (1827).

CHAPTER VIII

1 Edited by Stephen Lee and Leslie Stephen.

2 Clifford Bax, *Pretty Witty Nelly*. Not very authentic.

3 Narcissus Luttrell, *Brief Relation of State Affairs*. Vol. I, p. 18.

4 Harleian MSS. 7319. 269. Brit. Mus.

5 The Rate Books of this period are now kept by the Westminster City Public Library, Buckingham Palace Road.

6 *Survey of London*, Vol. XXIX. Anon Works. Part I. Much of this information is derived from this Survey.

7 Copies and photostats of these five deeds are with the Greater London Record Office, the County Hall. Ref. R.230–234.

8 Colley Cibber, *Apology for his Life*, Vol. II, p. 211.

9 John H. Wilson, *A Rake and his Times*.

10 *The Story of Nell Gwynne*, illustrated with Various Portraits, MSS. and bound letters, commenced 1884, finished and bound in 4 volumes by Zaehnsdorf, 1891.

11 Calendar of State Papers Venetian, 1671–1672.

CHAPTER IX

1 Harleian MSS. Brit. Mus. 7003. 216.

2 *Memoirs of John Evelyn, Comprising his Diary from 1641–1705/6*. Edited from the original MSS. by William Bray, Vol. II, p. 349.

3 The Manuscripts of St. George's Chapel, Vol. XI. These MSS. have been edited by John Neale (1957).

4 *Letters from the Marchioness de Sévignè to her daughter the Countess de Grignan*. Spurrier and Swift, p. 69, Vol. IV.

5 *Moneys Received and Paid for Secret Services of Charles II and James II 1680–1688*. Edited from a Manuscript in the possession of William Selby Lowndes.

6 Calendar of State Papers Venetian 1671–1673.

CHAPTER X

1 Cyril Hughes Hartmann, *The Vagabond Duchess* (1927).

2 *Correspondence Angleterre* 119, f. 1, French Archives, Quai D'Orsay. Courtin to Louis XIV, 2nd July 1676.
   Cyril Hughes Hartmann, *The Vagabond Duchess* (1927).

3 *Correspondence Angleterre*, folio 1.

4 Ibid., 120 C. 24th September 1676.

5 Ibid., 122, f. 52.

6 Ibid., 123, A. f. 120. 2nd February 1677.

7 Theophilus Lucas, *Lives of the Gamesters* (1714).

8 Ibid., p. 247.

9 Cyril Hughes Hartmann, *The Vagabond Duchess* (1927).

10 *Correspondence Angleterre*, 123 C. f. 24.

CHAPTER XI

1 Add. MSS., 27872, fol. 18, Brit. Mus.

2 Add. MSS., 27872, fol. 20, Brit. Mus.

3 H.M.C. Ormonde, MSS. Vol. IV.

4 Aff. Etr. Angleterre tome CXX, fol. 68; tome CXXXI, fol. 146 (1678).

5 Elizabeth D'Oyley, *James, Duke of Monmouth* (1938).

6 *Memoirs of the Verney Family, From the Restoration to the Revolution, 1660–1696*, Vol. IV, p. 265, 1679.

7 Hon. Henry Sidney, *Diary of the Times of Charles II*, including his Correspondence with the Countess of Sunderland.

8 H. M. C. Ormonde MSS., Vol. IV, p. 99.

9 Harleian MSS. 7319, f. 135. *An Essay of Scandal* (1681).

10 *The Rochester-Savile Letters, 1671–1680*, Edited by John Harold Wilson.

11 Harleian MSS., Brit. Mus. 7003, 216.

12 *The Rochester-Savile Letters 1671–1680*, Edited by John Harold Wilson.

13 Ibid.

14 Calendar of State Papers Venetian.

15 Harleian MSS., Brit. Mus. 7003, 283, 11th August 1677.

16 Stowe MSS. 211, f. 330. Brit. Mus.

17 *The Rochester-Savile Letters, 1671–1680*, Edited by John Harold Wilson.

18 Harleian MSS., Brit. Mus. 7003. 183.

M

CHAPTER XII

1 Peter Cunningham, *The Story of Nell Gwyn and the Sayings of Charles the Second.*

2 Bishop Gilbert Burnet, *The History of His Own Times*, Vol. I, p. 463.

3 Printed in *Camden Miscellany*, Vol. V. Mr. Tite's Collection of Autographs, p. 25.
   Laurence Hyde was created Earl of Rochester in 1682. John Wilmot, Earl of Rochester's son had died at age of eleven.

4 H. M. C. Calendar of MSS. Duke of Ormonde at Kilkenny (Now in National Liberary, Dublin). N.S. Vol. VI.

5 MS. 2423. National Library of Dublin. The Duke of Ormonde's son Thomas Earl of Ossory had been a valued Lord Chamberlain to Queen Catherine of Braganza, but had died (1680).

6 H. J. Oliver, *Sir Robert Howard 1626–1698* (1963).

7 H. M. C. Ormonde MSS. N.S., Vol. IV.

8 H. J. Oliver, *Sir Robert Howard 1626–1698* (1963).

9 H. M. C. Ormonde MSS. N.S., Vol. IV.

10 Ibid.; Also H. J. Oliver, *Sir Robert Howard 1626–1698* (1963).

11 *Luttrell's Diary*, Vol. 1, p. 62.

12 W. J. MacQueen Pope, *Theatre Royal, Drury Lane.*

CHAPTER XIII

1 Hore, *History of Newmarket.*

2 *Letters of Humphrey Prideaux, Sometimes Dean of Norwich to John Ellis 1674–1722*. Edited by Maunde Thompson, p. 101.

3 E. H. Plumptre, D.D., *The Life of Thomas Ken, D.D., Bishop of Bath and Wells*, Vol. I, pp. 157 & 158 (1885).

4 Ibid.

5 This story is related by Clifford Bax in *Pretty Witty Nelly* (1932).

6 The incident is related by Arthur Irwin Dasent in *The Private Life of Charles II.*

7 *Memoirs of John Evelyn*, comprising His Diary, from 1641 to 1705–6, Edited from the original MSS. by William Bray, Vol. III (1827).

8 *Memoirs of Sir John Reresby 1634–1689*, edited from the original MSS.

9 *Annals of Windsor*, Tighe and Davis, Vol. 2.

10 *Ellis Correspondence*. Letters during the years 1686, 1687, 1688 and addressed to John Ellis, Vol. I, p. 118.

11 Oliver Hedley, *Windsor Castle.*

12 *The Manuscripts of St. George's Chapel,* Vol. XI, No. 9.

13 Eva Scott, *Rupert Prince Palantine,* p. 363 (1899).

14 1681. Add. Charters 15, 862–15, 846. Brit. Mus.; also Cornelius Brown, *A History of Nottinghamshire* (1891).

15 Moneys Received and Paid for Secret Services of Charles II and James II. From 30th March 1675, to 25th December 1688.

16 *An Historical and Topographical Description of Chelsea and its Environs,* Vol. II, p. 257.

17 Arthur Irwin Dasent, *Nell Gwynne 1650–1687.*

18 *Memoirs of John Evelyn Comprising His Diary from 1641–1705/6.* Vol. III, p. 36.

19 Ibid.

20 Narcissus Luttrell, *Brief Relations,* Vol. I, p. 151.

21 *The Life and Times of Anthony à Wood, Antiquary of Oxford, 1632–1695, described by himself.* Collected from his Diaries and other Papers, by Andrew Clark, Vol. 2.

22 Bishop Burnet, *History of His Own Time,* Vol. I.

23 *Memoirs of Sir Richard Bulstrode,* pp. 384–6.

24 Forneron, *Louise de Kéroualle, Duchess of Portsmouth, 1649–1734.*

25 Calendar of State Papers Domestic Charles II. January 1679.

26 *The Memoirs of Thomas Bruce, 2nd Earl of Ailesbury.*

CHAPTER XIV

1 *Memoirs of John Evelyn Comprising his Diary from 1641 to 1705/6.* Edited from the original MSS. by William Bray, Vol. III, p. 126.

2 *Lord Macaulay's History of England,* Vol. I, p. 428.

3 Ibid., Vol. I, p. 429.

4 Bishop Burnet, Note to *The History of the Reign of Charles II,* Vol. 2, p. 468.
Correspondence Angleterre, Vol. 154. 110. Archives Quai D'Orsay.

5 Mentioned also by Arthur Irwin Dasent in his *Nell Gwynne, 1650–1687.*

6 *Correspondence Angleterre,* Vol. 154. 110. Archives Quai D'Orsay.

7 *Memoirs and Correspondence of John Evelyn,* Vol. III.

8 Add. MSS., Brit. Mus., 21,483, f. 27.

9 Ibid., 21,483, f. 28.

10 Monies Received and Paid for Secret Services of Charles II and James II from 30th March 1679, to 25th December 1688.

CHAPTER XV

1 *State Trials*, Vol. 12. 1687–1696.

2 Ibid.

3 Hester W. Chapman, *Great Villiers, a Study of George Villiers 2nd Duke of Buckingham, 1628–1687.*

4 Colley Cibber, *Apology for his Life*, with notes and supplement. Edited by Robert W. Lowe.

5 *Memoirs of John Evelyn Comprising his Diary from 1641 to 1705/6,* 21st March 1683. Dr. Tenison succeeded Archbishop Tillotson as Archbishop of Canterbury.

6 Ebbel and Phebe Hoff, *The Life and Times of Richard Lower Physiologist and Physician (1631–1699).*

7 *Brief Relations of State Affairs, 1678–1714,* Vol. I, p. 420.

BIBLIOGRAPHY

Contemporary Memoirs

Count Magalotti's account of the Travels of Cosmo the Third Grand Duke of Tuscany, through England during the reign of Charles II.

The History of His Own Time by Bishop Gilbert Burnet, Vol. I.

Correspondence of the Family of Hatton, being chiefly letters addressed to Christopher 1st Viscount Hatton, A.D. 1601–1704.

Memoirs of John Evelyn, Esq., F.R.S., comprising His Diary from 1641 to 1705–6. Vols. I, II and III.

Diary and Correspondence of Samuel Pepys, F.R.S., with a Life and Notes by Richard Braybrook, in 4 volumes.

Memoirs of Sir Richard Bulstrode.

The History of the Reign of Charles II, by Bishop Burnet, Vol. 2.

Brief Relation, Volume 1, by Narcissus Luttrell.

Letters of Humphrey Prideaux, sometime Dean of Norwich to John Ellis, 1674–1722, edited by Maude Thompson.

Ellis Correspondence. Letters during the years 1686, 1687, 1688 and addressed to John Ellis, Vol. I.

Diary of the Times of Charles II by the Hon. Henry Sidney, including his Correspondence with the Countess of Sunderland.

The Rochester–Savile Letters, 1671–80, edited by John Harold Wilson.

Memoirs of the Verney Family, from the Restoration to the Revolution 1660–1696.

Memoirs of Sir John Reresby 1634–89, edited from the original MSS.

Letters from the Marchioness de Sévigné to her daughter the Countess de Grignan, Vol. IV (Spurr and Swift, 1927).

A Character of Charles II by Sir George Savile (Marquis of Halifax).

The Life and Times of Anthony à Wood, Antiquary of Oxford 1632–1695, described by himself. Collected from his Diaries and other Papers.

An original edition *The English Monsieur*, a Comedy as it is acted at the Theatre Royal by His Majesty's Servants. By the Hon. James Howard.

History of England by Lord Macaulay, Vol. I.

Memoirs of the Count de Gramont by Anthony Hamilton.

Transactions in England for the last hundred years preceding the Revolution (1688) by James Welwood.

Some Passages in the Life and Death of John, Earl of Rochester by Bishop Gilbert Burnet (1680).

An Account of the English Dramatick Poets by Gerard Langbaine, Vol. IV (1691).

Manuscripts and Material in Archives

Calendar of State Papers Domestic, Charles II.

Calendar of State Papers, Venetian, 1671–1672.

Harleian MSS. 7319; B.M.

Stowe MSS. B.M.

Additional MSS. B.M.

Ashmolean MM.

Bodleian Library.

Knole MSS.

Photostats of five deeds referring to Nell Gwyn in the Greater London Record Office, the County Hall.

Correspondence Angleterre, Vols. 119–124, French Archives, Quai D'Orsay.

The Manuscripts of St. George's Chapel, Vols. X and XI, Windsor.

The Rate Books 1670 and 1671 Westminster City Public Library, Buckingham Palace Library.

H.M.C. Ormonde MSS, Volume IV.

H.M.C. Calendar of Manuscripts of Duke of Ormonde formerly at Kilkenny, now in the National Library of Dublin.

Camden Miscellany, Vol. V.

Mr. Tite's Collection of Autographs.

State Trials, 1687–96, Vol. 12.

The Archives of Messrs. Glyn, Mills the Bankers at No. 1 Fleet Street have letters relating to Nell Gwynn's Financial Affairs.

The Story of Nell Gwynne, Illustrated with Various Portraits, MSS. and letters commenced 1884, finished and bound in four volumes by Zaehnsdorf (1891).

Other Books Consulted

Nell Gwynne 1650–1687 by Arthur Irwin Dasent (1924).

Pretty Witty Nelly by Clifford Bax (1932).

Sayings of Charles II, King Charles II by Sir Arthur Bryant (1932).

Charles II. His Life and Likeness (1960).

Nell Gwyn, Royal Mistress by John Harold Wilson (1952).

Privileged Persons Four Seventeenth Century Studies by Hester Chapman (1966).

The Vagabond Duchess by Cyril Hughes Hartmann (1927).

Charles II and Madame by Cyril Hughes Hartmann (1934).

Article by Sir Charles Petrie about Nell Gwynne, published in the *London Illustrated News*, 14th January 1956.

Rival Sultanas, Nell Gwynn and Louise de Kéroualle, by H. Noel Williams.

Sir Charles Sedley 1639–1701 by V. de Sola Pinto.

Rake Rochester by Charles Norman (1955).

Cavalier and Puritan in the days of the Stuarts by Lady Newdigate-Newdigate (1901).

The Age of Candlelight by Beatrice Saunders (1959).

Commonwealth and Restoration Stage by Hotson (1928).

Dryden to Johnson. The Pelican Guide to English Literature, edited by Boris Ford.

The Restoration Theatre by Montagu Summers (1934).

Sir Robert Howard 1626–1698 by H. J. Oliver (1963).

Great Villiers, a Study of George Villiers Second Duke of Buckingham, 1628–87, by Hester W. Chapman.

Annals of Windsor, Vol. 2. Tighe and Davis.

James Duke of Monmouth by Elizabeth D'Oyley (1938).

Windsor Castle by Oliver Hedley.

Louise de Kéroualle Duchess of Portsmouth 1649–1734 by Forneron.

The Life of Thomas Ken, D.D., Bishop of Bath and Wells by E. H. Plumptre (1885).

The Private Life of Charles II by Arthur Irwin Dasent (1927).

History of Nottinghamshire by Cornelius Brown (1891).

Prince Palantine by Eve Scott (1899).

Apology for his Life by Colley Cibber. Vols. I and II.

England in the Reign of Charles II by David Ogg (1934).

1660 The Year of Restoration by Patrick Morah (1960).

A Rake and his Times by John W. Wilson.

The Dramatic Works of Dryden, Vols. I and II (The Nonesuch Press).

Dramatic Miscellanies, Consisting of Critical Observations on Several Plays of Shakespeare by Thomas Davies, Vol. III.

The Court Wits of the Restoration by J. H. Wilson (Princetown 1948).

The Court at Windsor by Christopher Hibbert (1964)

Theatre Royal, Drury Lane by W. J. MacQueen Pope.

Some Account of the English Stage from the Restoration in 1660–1830 by Genest in Ten Volumes, Vol. I.

Mary Rich Countess of Warwick 1625–78 by Charlotte Fell-Smith.

Lucy Walter, Wife or Mistress by Lord George Scott (1947).

Collected Works of John Wilmot Earl of Rochester (Nonesuch Press).

Notes and Queries, Vols. CXC III and other series.

INDEX

Orrery, Roger Royle, 1st Earl of,
Mustapha, 40; *The Black Prince*, 63,
64
Otway, Thomas, 86, 95, 96, 121
Oxford, 20, 21, 43, 146
Oxford, Aubrey de Vere, 20th Earl
of, 23, 161

P
Pegge, Catherine, 76, 130
Pembroke, Thomas Herbert, 8th Earl
of, 87, 165
Penn, Sir William, 42–3, 52
    William (son), 80
Pepys, Mrs. Elizabeth, 16, 48, 69, 72
    Samuel, *Diary, quoted*, 13, 14, 15,
    17; on the theatre, 31, 36, 39, 43,
    47–8, 63, 64, 67, 68, 69, 72; on Nell
    Gwyn, 32, 40, 46, 52, 59, 61, 62, 71
Plymouth, Charles Fitzcharles, Earl
of, 77
Portsmouth, Louise de Keroualle,
Duchess of, maid of honour to
Henrietta, 81; attracts Charles II,
82, 97, 98; her career as his mistress,
99–104, 106–15, 139, 150–1, 153,
154; unpopularity, 100, 106–7, 109,
125, 146; wealth, 104, 161; ambition, 106, 145; a rabid papist, 122;
lampooned by Rochester, 125–6;
encounter with a highwayman,
139; honoured by Louis XIV, 141;
in old age, described by Voltaire,
161
Potevine, upholsterer, 134, 141
Preston, Richard Graham, 1st Viscount, 96

Q
Quin, Anne (actress), 49, 63, 86

R
Reresby, Sir John, 101, 145
Rhodes, Richard, *Flora's Vagaries*, 55,
63
Richmond, Charles Lennox, Duke of

(1675), 90, 100, 145, 155
    Charles Stuart, 3rd (1660) Duke
    of, 79, 100
    Frances (Stewart), Duchess of,
    41, 43, 77, 79, 100
Rochester, Elizabeth (Malet), Coun-
tess of, 123
    Laurence Hyde, Earl of (1682),
    62, 89, 95, 117, 128, 130, 165
    John Wilmot, 2nd (1658) Earl of,
    122–3, 126–7; his *Panegyrick on
    Nelly*, 18, 21, 22, 33; epitaph on
    Charles II, 80; advice to Nell
    Gwyn, 124; lampoons on Duchess
    of Portsmouth, 125–6; mentioned,
    15, 30, 32, 47, 59, 67, 95
Ross, Madame, 22, 23
Rupert, Prince, 59, 74, 143

S
St. Albans, Charles Beauclerk, Lord
Burford, 1st Duke of (Nell Gwyn's
elder son), 20, 81, 89, 95, 96, 133,
135, 143, 155; his titles and offices,
90, 141, 144, 161; pension, 160;
Burford House settled on, 141; a
"pretty boy", 145; his religion, 160;
army service, and marriage, 161;
inheritance, 165, 166, 167
St. Albans, Diana (de Vere), Duchess
of, 161
Sanderson, Mrs. (actress, *m.* Thomas
Betterton), 59
Sandys, Lucy Hamilton, Lady, 95, 165
Savile, Henry, 67, 95, 96, 123, 124,
125, 129
Savoy Chapel, 163
Sawyer, Sir Robert, 165
Scrope, Sir Carr, 129, 130
Sedley, Catherine (later Countess of
Dorchester), 60, 61 n, 129, 149
    Sir Charles, 16, 31, 56, 57, 58, 59,
    60, 68, 73, 160; *The Mulberry
    Garden*, 67–8
    Katherine (Savage), Lady, 60